# Liminal Reality and Transformational Power

# Liminal Reality and Transformational Power

*Revised Edition*

## Transition, Renewal and Hope

## Timothy Carson

The Lutterworth Press

**The Lutterworth Press**
P.O. Box 60
Cambridge
CB1 2NT
United Kingdom

www.lutterworth.com
publishing@lutterworth.com

ISBN: 978 0 7188 9401 6

*British Library Cataloguing in Publication Data*
A record is available from the British Library

First published by
University Press of America®, Inc., 1997

Second edition published by
The Lutterworth Press, 2016

*For all those who have passed through life-shaking trauma*
*and found transformation on the other side*
*of the liminal wilderness*


Foxes have holes,
and birds of the air have nests;
but the Son of Man has nowhere
to lay his head.

MATTHEW 8:20

# Contents

# Foreword

The work which follows provides ample evidence that a call to parish ministry need not mean abandonment of the academic life. To the contrary, when serious theological work takes place, the parish is a rich context for the praxis of action and reflection.

This text models how the pursuit of knowledge may be explored and enhanced as the history of scholarship intersects with present human narratives.

Academics and pastors alike will find this study to be a definitive source for the depth issues surrounding liminality. It opens up new vistas as it discloses everything which pastoral epistemology can be.

*Dr. Peggy Brainard Way*
Professor of Pastoral Theology
Eden Theological Seminary
St. Louis, Missouri

# *Preface*

My original exploration into the power of liminal reality arose during work on a Doctor of Ministry dissertation at Eden Theological Seminary in St. Louis, Missouri. I am indebted to the faculty of Eden as well as broad scholarship and research found in diverse disciplines. My great thanks goes to Nancy Miller for her tireless copy editing of this edition. I also deeply appreciate the array of family members, friends, and colleagues who have encouraged me in my endeavor. They have shown me what love means in its most concrete form.

Writing a book and having it published is more like sowing seeds than anything else; one never knows where the ideas will take root or how they might flourish. When my work on liminality first hit the literary streets some eighteen years ago, I did not know who might read it or rely on it as a source for their own work. Because the book was first published by an academic press, it most often ended up living on the shelves of university libraries. That explains both its geographic reach as well as numerous citations among disparate academic disciplines.

The original emergence of liminality studies took place within the domains of anthropology and sociology. Various psychological schools of thought were close on their heels. Others, including theology and education, found and applied it later.

The categories of liminality have recently found fresh applications within the social and political sciences. With the arrival of the 100th anniversary of the publication of Arnold van Gennep's *Rites of Passage* in 1909, the journal *International Political Anthropology* published a special edition dedicated to the issue of liminality (issue 2, vol. 1, 2009). Out of that effort grew the anthology *Breaking Boundaries: Varieties of Liminality* which contains expansions of the earlier journal articles as well as newly written chapters.[1] Its focus is primarily on social, political and international dimensions.

The fact that liminal studies remain current and relevant a century after the publication of van Gennep's seminal book is a testimony to their staying power. Serious scholars and practitioners continue to find helpful tools that aid them in analysis and constructive approaches to transitional states and their resolution.

Of course, the life experience of any author accumulates over intervening years and brings with it inevitable shifts in perspective. That has certainly been true in my own case. But throughout that evolution of thought my appreciation for the central insights of liminality has remained relatively constant. That may have to do with the universal nature of liminal phenomena and how they are embedded in the fabric of life itself.

If I were to change the model of the book in any regard, it might be to rely less on a Hegelian idealism, with its sense of linear progression, and appeal more to process thought, which allows for novelty and chaos as a part of the unfolding. In addition, I also believe that it would be helpful to draw on the insights of quantum physics, insights that would certainly make a remarkable contribution in almost every liminal category. That project awaits the future brilliance of some creative doctoral student.

In this second edition, I have added one more chapter in the so-called "practical theology" section, the later part of the book that focuses on application of insights. As regards the ubiquitous nature of war in our own time, we are not exceptional or unique; many civilizations have experienced the same thing. But two current aspects are different. War itself is conducted in a very different form than it was only a century ago. In the West we also live in a particular cultural context in which returning warriors perish in epidemic numbers and in ways unrelated to battle. They are disproportionately dying after war has ended as the result of their own inner wounds. I firmly believe this is related to a certain rupture that may best be understood through liminal categories. It is to that concern that my additional words are addressed.

# Introduction

The door, the ladder, the crossing, the maze, the bridge between two river banks - these are but a few of the symbols of passage, initiation and transformation which speak of dangerous and essential journeys.

Huck Finn floats down the river, and we know he has entered another state of being; his life shall never again be the same, and his very identity stands suspended, having entered a different category of existence, time, and space. He floats between the two solid shores, and the river both suspends and transports his unfinished life to uncertain places.

Midway through life's journey, Dante strays from the predictable roads of his past only to find himself isolated in a dark wood. A wilderness fills him with dread, and yet, his entrance into these shadows precipitates a harrowing journey through the hellish and the heavenly, the human and the divine.

Upon the face of the deep Noah huddles in his ark, surrounded by pairs of opposites, waiting out the indeterminate forty days. The deep, the chaos holding its own power, lifts the seeds of a new world to the solidity of a land somehow different now, after its washing.

As the desert becomes an unchosen home for Moses and his followers, and one year stretches into forty years, that which seemed temporary now becomes permanent. The children of Israel live on a bridge between captivity and the blessings of promise. On that bridge they encounter the best and the worst, the realization of divine presence and temptation to its abandonment. Only wilderness yields promise. When Moses finally waves his people on, he himself stays behind. He does so knowing his grave will be planted on the soil where many will be transformed.

Not by choice does Elijah flee and hide. Crisis leads his course, and his flight is less noble than it is desperate. If forty days in the cave of despair brings anything to Elijah, it is not a revelation of the sacred engendered by the outer veneer of storm and earthquake; it brings, rather, a still, quiet, and distant voice, more like an echo than anything else.

Not unlike Noah floating toward his new world, Moses and the children of Israel making their way through wilderness, and Elijah re-entering the womb of his cave, Jesus is compelled to enter that place and time named forty, which is also his flood, his wilderness, and his womb of transformation. There he faces his own greatness and the temptations that are inherent in it. Wrestling with the deepest and most powerful instincts, impulses, and drives, his spirit is refined until he discerns and finally submits to his highest loyalty. Then, and only then, is Jesus forged into the One who may speak with authority of a realm, reign, and empire which cannot be seen here or there, but must be known within, among, hidden, coming, and already present. Whether encompassed in forty days or forty years, symbolic time and space are marked off for the most significant transitions and initiations of our humanity.

In the following pages, inquiry and exploration shall take us to that sacred place found between places, that sacred time found between the times, and to the transformative power which grows in this fertile field of what has come to be called the liminal.

Through the examination of transitional social rites and rituals and their corresponding patterns of interior states of being, this study attempts to elucidate the nature of liminal reality. Transitional phenomena hold inherent and potential transformative power. For people of faith, and especially those in roles of religious leadership, this suggests not only a hermeneutical key and a pastoral method: it suggests new ways of understanding the very identity of those who dare to stand at the critical intersections found somewhere between here and there.

*Part I*

# Chapter 1
# Anthropology and the Rites of Passage

It was at the turn of the Twentieth Century that anthropologist Arnold van Gennep identified broad patterns of regeneration within communal systems. From his observation of the cultural transitions of renewal which are given form through rites and ritual, he came to understand a particular genre of social transition that he named the *Rites of Passage*. This descriptive phrase became the title of his landmark book which was first published in 1909.[1]

Van Gennep came to believe that the energy found in any system eventually dissipates and must be renewed at crucial intervals. This renewal and transition is accomplished in the social milieu by various rites of passage. These rites not only foster transition but protect the social structure from undue duress and disturbance. Developmental life transitions necessitating rites of passage include pregnancy, childbirth, childhood, departure from childhood, puberty, betrothal-marriage and death. In addition, territorial transitions often require certain rites of passage as one moves physically from one geographic area to another. He "finds himself physically and magico-religiously in a special situation for a certain length of time: he wavers between two worlds."[2]

Rites of passage held great importance in the change of social status, movement between tribes and castes, and the progression of age. They also served a crucial purpose in remarkable but temporary events such as illness, dangers, journeys, and war. The rites of passage include ceremonies which mediate transition on all the most important occasions of life.[3] Though assuming different types of rites, he did not differentiate between them as clearly as would later elaboraters.[4]

Van Gennep defined the structure of the Rites of Passage in terms of the "preliminal," which includes separation from a previous world, a transitional period; and the "post-liminal," distinguished by "ceremonies of incorporation into the new world."[5] Unique among his contemporaries for observing not only the particularity of cultures, but also patterns of transition common

1

to them, he came to believe that the rites of passage, including separation, transition, and incorporation, vary little except in matters of detail.[6] The underlying structure is almost always the same. "Beneath a multiplicity of forms, either consciously expressed or merely implied, a typical pattern always recurs: the pattern of the rites of passage."[7]

For a scholar of his time, whose study centered upon the uniqueness of cultural forms as found in their own contexts, this was a remarkable and risky thesis. If the recognition of anything resembling structural universals was suspect in van Gennep's day among his peers, we could only expect it to be more so in our present post-modern atmosphere. With a heightened sensitivity to the ways in which dominant culture attempts to define what should be universal for all, especially for marginal groups on the periphery of power, there is an understandable inclination to question both perception and motive. As Robert Bellah reminds us, certain presumptions about knowing claim an objective knowledge as though it is "knowledge without a subject . . . context free, untouched by human hands, validated by its own methodological canons."[8] To the contrary, knowing subjects are not distinct from their world in a splendid objectivity; they are a part of the world they perceive. "Thus we could speak not of knowing subjects knowing a world, but of a world knowing itself through knowing subjects."[9] It is understandable why such a suspicion toward claims to universal knowledge is prevalent even when certain evidence might lead to more structuralist conclusions.

For van Gennep, though, structural commonality and distinctive cultural variety are not mutually exclusive; they co-exist and interact. Common patterns emerge in distinct and unique cultures. Life itself is described in terms of passage, and the rites of passage are the vehicles by which the great transitions are traversed. He frames this in the broadest terms:

> For groups as well as for individuals, life itself means to separate and to be reunited, to change form and condition, to die and be reborn. It is to act and to cease, to wait and rest, and to begin acting again, but in a different way. . . . And there are always new thresholds to cross: the thresholds of summer and winter, of a season or a year, of a month or a night; the thresholds of birth, adolescence, maturity, and old age; the threshold of death and that of the afterlife - for those who believe in it.[10]

At the annual meeting of the *American Ethnological Society* in Pittsburgh, March 1964, anthropologist Victor Turner presented a paper which both built on and extended beyond the previous work of van Gennep.[11] Presenting a model of society as a "structure of positions," Turner describes the liminal period as an "interstructural situation."[12]

The term liminal derives from the Latin, *limins,* and refers to the threshold passageway between two separate places. The liminal state is a transitional one; positioned between states determined by social place, status, maturity, socio-economic position, caste, physical location, mental or emotional condition, health, war and peace, scarcity or plenty.[13]

Formalized rites of passage are found primarily in the small, stable, cyclical societies relating to "biological and meteorological rhythms and recurrences rather than with technological innovations."[14] It is in such contexts that the three phases of the rites of passage - separation, limin, reaggregation may most clearly be seen. It is through the participation in this transitional process that one becomes transformed.[15] Life is characterized by the punctuation of "a number of critical moments of transition."[16]

In the first phase of transition in the rites of passage, that of *separation*, there is a time of detachment and detaching from the earlier period, place, or state in the cultural or social context. In the last phase of this process, the time of *aggregation*, there is a return to a stable position, one that is socially located but different from the former phase—a transformed, altered condition.

Between the beginning phase of separation and the concluding phase of aggregation, there is the *liminal*. This betwixt and between time is filled with ambiguity. This liminal phase lacks past coordinates, without the form and structure which is to be.

The person who is moving through the rites of passage, the "transitional being" or "liminal personae," is defined by "a name and by a set of symbols."[17] The condition is one of ambiguity and paradox, betwixt and between states of being assigned by convention, "a confusion of all the customary categories."[18]

One of the characteristics of the transitional or liminal being is that of ritual uncleanliness. Turner includes the insights of anthropologist Mary Douglas to give the clearest exposition of the polluting qualities of the transitional being, as they are neither one thing or another. "Liminal personae nearly always and everywhere are regarded as polluting to those who have never been . . . 'inoculated' against them, through having been themselves initiated into the same state."[19]

In Douglas's own work, she relates the observations of social anthropology regarding the concepts of pollution and taboo to the liminal state. The concept of hygiene and defilement is the key to understanding order and disorder; being and non-being; form and formlessness; life and death in ancient societies.[20]

Within the idea of contagion there is an inherent avoidance of defilement. Rituals of purity regulate order and unity in experience and society. Because persons within a liminal state are presently placeless, their status is indefinable.[21] Danger is present in this transitional state, "simply because transition is neither one state nor the next. . . . The person who must pass from one to another is . . . in danger and emanates danger to others."[22] Prescribed rituals control the danger through physical and symbolic separation and segregation from the larger community until a public entry into a new status takes place. During this most dangerous separated phase, this liminal period of separation for protection and passage, the novice or initiate is temporarily outcast. Ironically, to exist at the dangerous margins is also to touch a unique source of power.[23] Hence the liminal state is simultaneously dangerous, polluted, potentially contaminating, as well as power-filled and the source of mysterious fascination.

Indeed, the liminal state is so dangerous and its passage so delicate that careful attention must be given to liminal behaviors; they serve a crucial role in safe passage. The tribe, therefore, gives great attention to its totem and accompanying eating prohibitions related to particular genus and species. There exists a symbolic power which may interfere with transformation.[24]

Turner's well-known and cited work, *The Ritual Process: Structure and Anti-Structure,*[25] further develops his analysis of the liminal personae. Life within a community is a type of dialectical process, one which moves between structure and anti-structure with each individual alternating between these poles by means of transitions to new and changing states.[26] Therefore, the attributes of the liminal personae, by virtue of their very transitional nature, stand in binary opposition to established structure. As distinctions of structure are suspended, liminal entities take upon themselves symbolic, transitional status and particular attributes: nothingness, sexlessness, anonymity, submissiveness and silence, and sexual continence.[27]

A special camaraderie develops among those sharing liminal passages. Turner has called this special bond between liminal persons *"communitas."* This is a bond which transcends any socially established differentiations. Those who share the liminal passage develop a community of the inbetween. This creates a community of anti-structure whose bond continues even after the liminal period is concluded. A significant sharing of the liminal passage creates strong egalitarian ties which level out differences in status and station which have been established by structure.[28]

If an individual within a social system fluctuates, as does the system itself, between structure and anti-structure, rituals in the form of rites of passage negotiate complicated and conflicted relationships. As Catherine Bell describes it, ritual operates as a mechanism "for the resolution of basic oppositions or contradictions."[29] Ritual belongs to a category of experience, but it also is an important form of analysis, an interpretive key by which one may understand culture and the ways in which people make and re-make their worlds. As in other rituals, rites of passage are based on two structural patterns: an activity and the fusion of thoughts and beliefs with that activity.[30] As a thought-action dichotomy, ritual functions to create solidarity, negotiate or repress either change or conflict, and define reality itself.[31]

# Chapter 2
# Life, Death and Rebirth

As the discipline of anthropology identified transcultural rites of passage, the liminal state of being, and peculiar liminal relationships forming egalitarian communitas, it was joined by the history of religions school and the study of mythic systems. The rites of passage and liminal reality have always been part of larger religious understandings of transformation which include these same personal and social structures. Religious epistemology, though, includes awareness of the sacredness of such states of being and insists that such experience cannot be interpreted apart from it.

Even as his contemporary, Arnold van Gennep, was writing about the rites of passage and their deep, commonly shared structures, Emile Durkheim was relating these very same anthropological observations to the sociology of religious experience.[1] Durkheim argued that the religious dimension of reality is an indispensable part of the social, rather than one positioned over and against it. In terms of both form and function, rites of passage, and the corresponding state of liminality, bridge the oppositional realities which have been called sacred and profane.

> The sacred and the profane have always and everywhere been conceived by the human mind as two distinct classes, as two worlds between which there is nothing in common. . . . This is not equivalent to saying that a being can never pass from one of these worlds into the other: but the manner in which this passage is effected, when it does take place, puts into relief the essential duality of the two kingdoms. In fact it implies a veritable metamorphosis. This is notably demonstrated by initiation rites, such as they are practiced by a multitude of peoples.[2]

In rites and rituals of transformation, one is not only attaining a new status within the social system, though it is most certainly that; there is a change of being itself, an ontological passage. In terms of a person sharing in such an initiation rite, there is a

transformation totius substantae—of the whole being. It is said that at
this moment . . . the person [who] was ceases to exist, and that another
is instantly substituted for it. He is re-born under a new form. . . . Does
this not prove that between the profane being which . . . was and the
religious being which . . . becomes, there is a break of continuity?[3]

From the religio-symbolic perspective, all of the rites of passage are
passages of death and rebirth leading participants into another form of
existence. Time and space is thereby interpreted in light of sacred categories.
Liminal existence is located in designated, separated, sacred space, frequently
representing connection to the earth and the divine. Moses treads on holy
ground (Ex. 3:5); Isaiah cowers in the temple of holiness (Is. 6:1-6); and
Jacob's dream floats somewhere between earth and heaven (Gen. 28:12-19).

Sacred time takes place as a separation from secular continuities, breaking
with simple chronology and the meanings that chronology holds. It is created
through the repetition of periodic dramatizations throughout a liturgical
cycle. Meaning is patterned through a ritualized, formalized procession
of symbols or symbolic actions. And for participants, this alternate time
becomes constituent of both this dramatic movement and symbolic content.[4]

Mircea Eliade places the locus of the revelation of sacred knowledge in
the sacred space and time of the liminal state.[5] Liminal existence in sacred
time and space is the preeminent setting in which revelation takes place,
knowledge is imparted, and consciousness changed. As the sacred time
and space is filled with the experience of darkness, death, and the nearness
of divine terror, the initiatory experience of death is often expressed
mythologically in various stories of descent to the underworld, inner
places, and womb-like spaces.[6] Ecstatic experience often accompanies the
experience of the soul's flight to heaven as well as to subterranean locales.[7]
In a contemporary parallel, liminal space and time have been identified
as the usual locales in which evangelical revival, with its goals of personal
conversion and transformation, was located.[8]

The content of liminal revelation is usually three-fold: "revelation of
the sacred, of death, and of sexuality."[9] This informs and gives form to
the symbolism of initiations where "birth is almost always found side by
side with that of death."[10] Initiation rituals often hold the well-known
symbolism "implying a regressus ad uterum. . . . From the archaic stages
of culture the initiation of adolescents includes a series of rites whose
symbolism is crystal clear: through them the novice is first transformed into
an embryo and then is reborn. Initiation is equivalent to a second birth.
It is through the agency of initiation that the adolescent becomes both a
socially responsible and culturally awakened being."[11] This corresponds to
"the reversion of the universe to the 'chaotic' or embryonic state,"[12] bringing
about a "mystical rebirth, spiritual in nature in other words, access to a new

mode of existence."[13] The initiation ceremony inevitably includes a three-fold schema: suffering, death, and resurrection. By implication, ritual solitude and symbolic death are represented in almost all initiation ceremonies."[14]

Patterns inherent in the rites of passage are frequently found within the patterns of transformation in the mythic systems of the world's religions. The liminal state is a place of sacred time and space, set apart and separated, the locus of revelation. The mythic journey and the corresponding rites usually rely on the symbolism of death and birth, fraught with conflict and often cosmic in scope.

Though Durkheim and Eliade have dealt with the concept of the sacred in complementary ways, defining it as a category of existence which is separated from the profane, they stand in polar opposition in terms of their explanations of the origin and nature of that sacred time. For Durkheim, the sacred was the sacralisation of the social, the projection of basic categories of thought and guiding ideas onto the religious plane.[15] In theological study this understanding was first given its clearest expression by Feuerbach, though for different reasons and with a differing anthropology.[16] This would be developed to its logical conclusion later, most obviously by the existentialists, and, of course, Marx.

For Eliade, the distinction between the sacred and the profane is found in the contrast between two entirely different types of time. Sacred time transcends and even denies the definitive character of historical event as it returns to primeval states of being. The sacred exists in a timeless, spaceless world.[17]

The polarities are created between the absoluteness of Eliade's sacred and the relativity of Durkheim's sacred. The sacred of Eliade is socially irrelevant, unbound by space and time. As such it can never serve as a correlational model for social life. The sacred of Durkheim is related to time and space as it forms a sacred model of society.[18]

At this seam of the sacred, this point of confusion where the social and the divine collide, the interval of tension between the Durkheimian and Eliadean sacreds, Turner brings a fusion between oppositions in the concept of liminality. In both cases sacred time and space is liminal. And according to Turner, both timelessness and chronological time, social space and space beyond social categories are all included in the liminal reality of the rites of passage. There is a certain timelessness and return to the beginnings of time, an unmediated contact between the individual and the divine. And yet the rites as a whole are very interested with creating and recreating social beings who will live in actual human communities. The Durkheimian and Eliadean elements are inter-dependent, creating a form of the sacred which paradoxically and simultaneously affirms and denies the importance of the social. "They are plays upon the contrast between the social and the divine."[19]

In the symbolism of the Christian narrative, the transformational patterns are found in the motifs of the descending/ascending redeemer who, separated from origins, passes through the liminal period of suffering and crucifixion only to experience resurrection and transformation while ushered into a new state of existence. Through belief and the act of religious imagination, the Christian is identified with the redeemer and the power of the transformational narrative. Baptismal rites, particularly those Pauline in form and origin, reflect the believer's identification with the death and resurrection of Christ. In a liminal moment between an old sin-ruled self which is dominated by death, the initiate plunges into the tomb, the womb, the watery chaos of baptism, only to emerge never to know death again. Knowing death with Christ, there is knowledge of life in and participation with Christ (Romans 6:1-14). This new state of being is shared in communitas with others who have shared this same liminal initiation, having passed through death into life (I Corinthians 12:12-27). Their lives are enfolded in a different form of existence; there is neither slave nor free, male nor female, Jew nor Gentile. All drink of the same spirit, part of the same body of Christ (Galatians 3:27-28).

As a hermeneutical key, this schema of transformation has been adapted in the service of historical studies, narrative criticism, liturgical and ritual studies and other related fields. Though a helpful model, caution must be used in adapting it too freely in the service of solving many of the analytical problems of other disciplines.[20]

# Chapter 3
# On Being There all the Time

In the practice of many world religions and religious movements, the liminal state of being and its corresponding creation of communitas comes to be pursued as a permanent condition. The most remarkable example is found in the highly developed monastic traditions of separation and communal life. Turner identifies monastic life as a form of permanent liminality which attempts to maintain the aspects of liminal reality for indefinite periods. The resulting communitas created by this permanent liminal state fosters characteristics of self-discipline, humility and obedience to authority, sexual abstinence, restraint in conversation, homogeneity, equality, anonymity, absence of property, elimination of status levels, uniform apparel, and minimalization of gender distinctions.[1]

The figure of St. Francis of Assisi is a prime example of a person who embodies permanent liminality. The beginning and end of his ministry is framed by nakedness, both in his conversion to his call and at his death, as a master symbol of the suspension of kinship rights, possession of property, simplicity and social disestablishment.[2] Indeed, the same qualities and characteristics are found in the many narratives of wandering holy people and saints, as well as founders of set-apart movements located in the structural margins of society and world. These movements place or find themselves in a liminal state of symbolic time: a time between the times, suspended between the present and future.[3]

Movements which are set over and against dominant or prevailing culture, in positions of anti-structure, frequently emerge at critical junctures and boundaries when social foundational plates are shifting or in direct conflict. In the analysis of such movements, Phillas Maack identifies liminal characteristics expressed in a shared communitas:

> All set themselves against social and political structures and parties, and all, to different degrees, preached nonviolence and poverty. Most early followers wore uniform dress and practiced symbolic acts of self-abnegation and communality. Francis, the Quakers, and Gandhi stripped naked; Francis and Gandhi tended lepers; Fox tended the mad.[4]

Interestingly, persons who share liminal states in communitas are sometimes there for altogether different reasons. There are those who choose a permanent state of liminality, and others who are liminal by circumstance, condition, or social definition. The liminal personae comes to be in two ways, the voluntary and involuntary. It is not uncommon for the former to gravitate to the latter. Perhaps the same impulse which leads one to enter such a state leads one toward a compassion for those who may have no such choice. The longing to enter the limins may be coupled with an empathy for those who are already there through no freedom or moral agency of their own. Though one may not personally experience the kinds of circumstances which lead to an involuntary liminality, one may know liminal reality by choosing to enter another form of it. This may be sufficient for creating a shared communitas.

Certainly the Christological theme of servanthood includes a vocation of emptying the self for the sake of those already empty by condition. At the very least this includes a willingness to surrender oneself for the sake of those in the margins.

Permanent liminality is not only found in established communities, but is uniquely embodied in itinerancy. As a betwixt and between interim state of being, itinerancy was highly characteristic of the Jesus movement.[5] In placing the Jesus movement and its practice of itinerancy in its social context, John Dominic Crossan has related this liminal phenomenon to the Greco-Roman Cynic tradition. He believes that the Cynics formed a basis of influence not only for the Jesus movement, but also for later Christian monasticism as well. Cynicism included a renunciation of the values of the world and society and a radical form of social protest. This protest included a refutation and a rejection of possessions or permanent responsibilities. It was, in essence, a philosophy of withdrawal and distance.[6]

The inner logic of Cynic philosophic thought hinged on the relationship of poverty to freedom; the former brings the latter. It is poverty which frees one from slavery to structure, and the only way to true royalty is such freedom.[7] The standard uniform of the Cynic included the cloak, bag and staff, the symbolic epitome of itinerancy. Their barefooted itinerancy included indigence, sleeping on the ground or in the baths or public buildings as vagrants.[8] Their diet consisted of water and vegetables, they begged in the market places, did not cut their hair or beards, and wore deliberate anti-social symbolic dress. All of this expressed emancipation from the systems of the Empire.[9] Cynics created and maintained a permanent liminality positioned in the locale of anti-structure and lived the characteristics belonging to the liminal personae.

Against those who place Jesus more centrally in the prophetic tradition of Judaism, Crossan describes Jesus as a "Peasant Jewish Cynic."[10] Though sharing many of the Cynic practices, Jesus and his disciples were primarily rural and communal; Cynics centered in urban areas and market places, functioning in a solitary way.[11] In common with the Cynics was the radical egalitarianism of Jesus which was expressed most clearly in free healing and common meals with all manner of socially stationed persons. This radical critique of the Roman patronage system and Jewish religious structures was a hallmark of his understanding of the realm and reign of God, which was unmediated contact with God and one another.[12]

Communitas in the Jesus movement existed among permanent itinerants living betwixt and between worlds according to time and location and existing in radical anti-structure. Indeed, these liminal persons would be joined to one another in ways which transcended even family relationship (Mark 3:31-35). It is in the liminal state of itinerancy and the resulting communitas that the Empire of God, so different from the Empire of Rome, may be known, preached, and lived.

If itinerancy as a form of permanent liminal existence was characteristic of the Jesus movement, it was equally so in the earliest forms of Palestinian Christianity. Gerd Theissen argues that in the same way Jesus lived an itinerant ministry, so he "called into being a movement of wandering charismatics."[13]

These wandering charismatics and local, established communities shared a reciprocal need for one another; the itinerant disciples provided preaching, teaching, and healing, as local communities provided hospitality. Disciples depended on this hospitality, as a sign of the benevolence and care of God (Mark 6:6b-13).

> The decisive figures in early Christianity were travelling apostles, prophets, and disciples who moved from place to place and could rely on small groups of sympathizers in these places.[14]

Liminal characteristics parallel to those of the itinerant Jesus movement and Greco-Roman Cynicism include lack of home, family, possessions, and protection. This wandering itinerancy is only possible as a movement of outsiders, since persons of position holding home, family, possessions, and security are settled and domesticated. In contrast, these itinerants "lived as those who expected the end of the world."[15] Paradoxically, the liminal must depend upon the non-liminal for support. And yet, those in settled communities not only seek, but need what the itinerants have to offer.

This same "itinerant radicalism" is found particularly in Thomas Christianity, a movement of wandering radicalism in earliest Gnostic Christianity.[16] Steve Patterson follows and expands upon Theissen in recognizing the reciprocal partnership between wandering charismatics and local sympathizers. The familiar pattern reappears: homeless radicals without family, wealth, or material possessions, wandering, preaching, and healing in exchange for hospitality. Local communities exist in a "mutually supportive relationship," providing food and shelter in exchange for preaching and healing.[17] As the liminal personae has a qualitatively different role and charmed existence, so the itinerant preacher has a different, charmed, and special status in relationship to the settled communities.[18]

The itinerant comes foremost as the stranger. The very root of this English word stranger is *strange:* other, different, or unknown. In the old French, *estrange* connotes the extraordinary. In Hebrew the word for stranger, *zur,* is found in the description of the edge or border of priestly items (Ex. 28:31-35). The stranger is the one emerging from beyond and living at the limins—the edge, border, threshold, and boundary. As one living at the liminal edge, the itinerant stranger is at once dangerous and fascinating. As the liminal personae is ambiguous, response to such a presence is confused and mixed.

In the Hebrew scriptures there exists the record of a far-ranging response to the presence of the stranger. Relating to their own historical identities as aliens, sojourners, and strangers, ancient Hebrews show remarkable concern for the stranger. One must love the stranger, even as one was a stranger (Deut. 10:19). Love and compassion for strangers stand as virtues and evidence of righteousness (Job 31:32). One of the harshest moral indictments includes injury of the most helpless—widows, orphans, and strangers (Ps. 94:6).

A profound fearfulness accompanies this ethic of moral obligation toward the stranger. As in most cultures, the foreigner, the homeless, and the displaced evoke fear and dread that one may become like them. Indeed, to become a stranger to one's own family or tribe represents an unrivaled state of misery (Ps. 69:8). The social status of the stranger is clearly less than established members of the community or family (Sir. 29:27). And in the wisdom literature, anything less than prudent caution in regard to strangers, especially in financial affairs, is the beginning of foolishness (Prov. 11:15).

In concert with the early strain of ethical concern for the stranger found in the Hebrew narratives, and in contrast to a simultaneous mistrust of them, much of Christian scripture and tradition exhibits remarkable compassion and concern. The very fabric of the Jesus movement, early Palestinian Christianity, and the missionary movement of the first generation is dependent on itinerancy and requisite hospitality. In addition, a remarkable and ultimate eschatological claim is made for the stranger. Not only are strangers to receive compassion, but their special status relates them to the moral significance of the sacred itself. To love the stranger is to love God. Indeed, this kind of love serves as an unexpected standard of judgment and mercy itself (Matt. 25:44). As opposed to dread of becoming a stranger, one is to seek this state of being, to become a *ho paragon,* a passer-by, as the way to God itself (Gos. Thomas log. 42).

As authority in established communities increasingly became vested in local authorities, the authority of anti-structure itinerants diminished, often eventuating in competition and even conflict.[19] As opposed to the communities of the Synoptic Gospels, established and establishing,[20] and closer to the wandering itinerants of early Palestinian Christianity, the "Thomas Christians too are homeless vagabonds, who have given up possessions and family ties. Like the wandering charismatics . . . , they have rejected conventional piety and its attitudes, and seem resistant to stringent organization."[21]

In Thomas Christianity, the rigors of itinerancy and the liminal status it conveyed found its theological expression in the Gnostic mythos, with its concept of the alien out of place in the created world.[22] For Thomas Christians, liminality became more than the structure of a social relationship; it is found in the very core of a belief system, tied to the nature of being and existence itself. What is at issue is the ontological condition as seen from the inside of the mythos itself.

As Ingvild Gilhus observes, "Gnostic religion furnishes a parallel to that type of permanent liminality."[23] Gilhus draws a strong connection between the intermediate realm of the archons—the middle stage in the Gnostic cosmos through which one must pass, either from the pneumatic world above to the material world below, or in return from the world below to that above—to the liminal phase of the Rites of Passage.[24] Existence itself is permanently liminal, lived in the intermediate realm. Itinerancy, then, is more than a choice; it is the historical expression of an ontological state of being. Since transformation takes place in the liminal phase, and existence is itself permanently liminal, the Gnostic mythos "is a mythology of passage."[25] As in other mythologies, the liminal state of being is that in which gnosis is communicated and serves as the locus of revelation. And life may be conceived as a period of permanent liminality.

The foundation of Gnostic communitas is its position of anti-structure, which often includes a separation from family ties and an abolition of structural status distinctions. It may include an antinomian character and liberty as regards law, though just as often it expresses itself in extreme asceticism, which is also a form of anti-structure.[26] Within the community of anti-structure, the community of the liminal, there exists a common life guided by internal equality, as the community shares the same structural position in a commonly-held mythos.[27] So the community realizes the principle of commonly shared property, as well as a leadership emerging from the charisms of the people, rather than hierarchical authority structures.[28]

> Gnostic religion is founded upon a tension between spirit and matter. . . . The conflict between being in God and not being in God is systematized in the gnostic myths of passage and is expressed through different levels of existence, with the spiritual world above and the material world below symbolizing the two polar states of being, and with the intermediate realm of liminality between.[29]

It is a common feature of mysticism in many places, times, and traditions that the mystic provisionally separates from established communities and religious structures. This separation is either temporary—immediately preceding the mystical experience with a return immediately forthcoming— or permanent. This allows them to return to their society to speak an authoritative word from the other side of their intense experience with the Holy. The identity of such a person is most usually set over and against the established community and prevailing religious authority, though remaining in some direct or indirect relationship to it. Even as the dominant thought of any time often generates its own countercurrents, so mystical experience and expression have often run parallel to their more discursive and rationalistic theological cousins. Itinerancy becomes for them the social expression of complex, intricate relationships which may remain in a creative tension.

A remarkable example from the medieval period is found in the Jewish *maskilim,* an order of mendicant kabbalists. With their purpose and role provided for and formalized in the Zohar, this itinerant mystical fellowship wanders the districts of the Galilee. They share their contemplative visions with a society from which they keep a sanctified distance.[30] Likewise, this theme becomes important among the early *Hasidim* of Eastern Europe as the lives of holy people are characterized by itinerant wandering and rootlessness.[31]

# Chapter 4
# The Inside of the Outside

The frequent parallel to and interior reflection of the liminal state found in rites of transformation and passage is an intra-psychic state of ecstatic experience. Though a dominance of rationalism and empiricism may depreciate the varied dimensions of non-rational ecstatic experience, an enlarged epistemology not only recognizes the importance of ecstatic experience, but also its direct relationship to liminal states of being. Ecstatic experience, especially when located in liminal passage, may be revelatory and provide special access to certain categories of knowing. In addition, ecstatic experience itself may be considered liminal as it constitutes an intra-psychic and interim phase of separation from the rational, perceiving ego. This separated anti-structure of the non-rational way of knowing moves to a post-liminal structure of rationality again, but in its transformed state it blends the insights of both rational and non-rational categories of knowing.

In primitive initiation ceremonies, the three-fold schema of suffering, death, and resurrection is dramatized externally through ritual solitude and symbolic death; the dreams and ecstasies which are frequently part of this rite not only usher the initiate into new knowledge of the sacred, but into a new religious social status.[1]

However infrequently religious ecstasy is mentioned as a feature of the apostle Paul's experience, it did play an important part in his spiritual transformation. As heavenly journeys served as means of claiming divine authentication, Paul shared past ecstatic experience with the Corinthian community in order to validate himself in competition with rivals.[2] Speaking of himself in the third person, he speaks of being "caught up to the third heaven" (2 Cor. 12:2a) in a state of dissociation from his body (12:2b, 3b). The holiness of his mystical experience was unexplainable, and the things which he experienced were beyond description (12:4).

In many cultures, a defining ecstatic experience sets apart persons as visionary spiritual leaders and healers. Though their experience might be described as psychotic within certain schools of thought, it is not at all to be considered psychopathological within the culture in which it is found; quite to the contrary, their culture venerates them because of the psychic journeys in which they have participated, and from which they draw their spiritual depth and authority.[3] Indeed, the founders, leaders, and spiritual guides of many religious movements, those who hold an exceptionally sensitive religious consciousness, have often lived at the boundary of the rational. This status was not a liability, but rather the very dynamic which enabled their ascent to great religious roles.[4] The images which come out of this ecstatic state and alternate way of knowing are not simply illusory; they correspond to meaningful reality of a different order.[5] Indeed, "Madmen are the children of God."[6]

In Michel Foucault's book, *Madness and Civilization,* he identifies the ways in which societies define what does and does not constitute madness or insanity.[7] Madness is reality which receives its meaning from the world-view of any given culture at any given moment in its development. Almost always defined as over and against the dominant culture and the prevailing anthropology, persons are evaluated according to commonly held symbolic codes, norms, and guiding ideas which comprise the good life and good society. As these presuppositions change and mutate, so do the definitions of what comprises madness, what madness means, and what measures will be used to deal with the madness.

In most pre-modern societies, there were provisions for and understanding of those persons who were charmed by a special, however unusual, perception of the world. Foucault documents a waning tolerance toward such persons during the 17th and 18th centuries. He relates the new intolerance to an emerging definition of human worth based upon the presence or absence of reason and rationality. These become the new criteria by which ultimate value is determined.

In the High Middle Ages, there was in place a vast network of leprosariums. By isolating infected persons, the disease declined dramatically, so much so that most leprosariums became uninhabited or abandoned. During the rise of this form of rationalism in the modern era, the attitudes formerly applied to leprosy were transferred to madness. Whereas in the Middle Ages mad people were integrated fairly normally into the mainstream of common life, an important shift took place in the 17th century. In the beginning, exclusion or banishment became the treatment of choice. Finally, in the classical period, confinement came into vogue with insane asylums taking the place, often literally, of the leprosariums.

Confinement emerges as a social phenomenon to deal with insanity. Foucault relates the rise of this social mechanism to a hiding of the unreasonable and irrational, especially as immorality became directly tied to the unreasonable.[8] This change redefined madness in its entirety:

> Madness in the classical period ceased to be the sign of another world, and it became the paradoxical manifestation of non-being.[9]

Indeed, it assumed a moral status which could only be construed in the most pejorative terms:

> Because madness became, in the classical period, a fearful expression of the absence of reason and omnipresence of animal drive, confinement was an attempt to 'annihilate nothingness.'[10]

As liminal personae, the mad are cast into a state of permanent liminality, cast off to sea in the "Ship of Fools," a community of the insane in permanent exile. This expulsion of insane members of society is a ritual exile which has to do, to a great extent, with avoidance of pollution and its accompanying danger. Water not only carries away, but has the symbolism of purification.[11] The society protects itself by exiling the pollutants in order that it may feel safe, secure, clean, and sane. Those who are excluded and cast into permanent anti-structure always live between two shores. In contrast to an earlier time when their delusions held a charmed status, strangely mediating things of a supernatural order, they float much like garbage barges today, refuse-in-exile, with no port to call home.

In his phenominological study of religious experience, William James gave special attention to and sympathetic descriptions of religious ecstasy and mystical states, though he did not share in these experiences personally.[12] What might be called a "nervous instability" is really normative for particular religious leaders who had an "exalted emotional sensibility . . . had frequently fallen into trances, heard voices, seen visions, and presented all sorts of peculiarities which are ordinarily classed as pathological."[13] George Fox was such a person of remarkable intellectual and spiritual capacity, and yet his was a life holding visions and ecstatic experience which defied rational categories.[14]

Rejecting the psychopathological assessment of this peculiarly religious phenomena, James ties it more closely to normative mystical states of consciousness.[15] Mystical states characterized by their ineffability which defies expression, noetic quality which transcends discursive rationality and reason, transiency and short duration, and passivity as the participant feels acted on more than acting.[16] As alternative forms of knowing, ecstatic and mystical states take their place alongside rational consciousness, which is itself but one form of knowing consciousness.[17]

These intra-psychic ecstatic states are liminal not only in the way they function in the middle phases of the rites of passage, but also as they act internally as passages of anti-structure over and against the structure of rationality. A whole new being becomes possible. Such religiously oriented and grounded states play an important role in the creation and formation of communitas by the way in which they relate to liminal passages in their own communal and cultural settings. Communitas is related directly to ecstatic liminal experience, because theirs is a sociology of ecstasy, a relating of the ecstatic to the social order.

Ioan Lewis places what he sees as the universality of mystical experience, including its language, symbolism, and dissociative trance states in the context of cultural interpretation of its meaning.[18] As such, it is not the province of those outside a particular culture and its interpretation to assess whether or not a person is actually "possessed." In opposition to such persons as Freud, who would classify such states, especially among what has been called primitive cultures, as expressions of pathological conditions, Lewis presents such phenomena as normal and accepted in the societies in which they are found.

> The reality of possession by spirits . . . constitutes an integral part of
> the total system of religious ideas and assumptions. Simply because we
> do not share their fantasies and find them echoed only in those whom
> in our own society we label psychotic or mentally deranged, gives us no
> warrant to write (them) off as mad. . . .[19]

Entry into ecstatic and mystical experience, especially in initiatory rites of passage, represents an involuntary surrender to disorder, a thrust into the chaos which is set over and against the ordered and controlled life of society. Such participation in liminal disorder claims the mystical participant, marking him or her with the transcendent. Liminal ecstatic experience draws one away from society into isolation, and exposes one to the very forces which may both threaten and transform the community.[20] Far from being pathological, ecstatic experience, possession, and other forms of psychic states are more rightly understood as "pre-scientfic psychotherapy," with spirits used to "explain what we regard as psychological states."[21]

Certainly, the most recent observations by the *American Psychiatric Association* toward Dissociative Disorders recognize a cross-cultural perspective: such experiences "can be a part of meditative practices that are prevalent in many religions and cultures, and should not be diagnosed as a disorder."[22]

To the contrary, intra-psychic altered states of consciousness represent the liminal phase of passage which is at the heart of all mystical experience. The essence of the interior passage is a movement from one metaphorical place to another in a crossing of the limins. For Bonaventure, this passage meant "The raising of the mind to God through the desire of love."[23] Teresa of Avila found this journey to be a movement beyond borders to a different locale: "the soul is completely suspended in such a way that it seems to be completely outside itself."[24] John of the Cross describes the liminal moment of contemplation as the place in which secret wisdom is "communicated and infused into the soul through love."[25] According to Evelyn Underhill, "It is an ordered movement towards ever higher levels of reality, ever closer identification with the infinite."[26] Though much has been recorded about mystical states and psychotic experience, including similarities as well as difficulties in discerning between them, little actual research has been conducted to develop ways to discriminate between their relatively similar characteristics. The research which has been done in this area discriminates between mystical states and psychotic experience not on the basis of subjective experience but rather according to personality structure and maturity.[27]

So the apostle's distinction between ecstatic experience and religious truth claims; the content of these claims acts as the measure of ecstatic states, and not the other way around (1 Corinthians 12:1-3). Indeed, the highest gift, *agape,* transcends any subjective experience (1 Corinthians 13:1).

Expanded and deepened communitas is found among communities that collectively share frequent dissociative and ritual trance states in the midst of corporate worship services. In Robert Fishman's research with the Unity Science Church, in Buffalo, New York, he found that spiritualist ritual acts as a mechanism to promote the multi-faceted wholeness of the entire community:

> Much of this is accomplished through the creation of a liminal state that allows believers to experience the alternative reality of the spiritual world, which forms the basis of their belief system. . . . The creation of a liminal state and accompanying transmigration experience is accomplished during the church service and culminates with the healing and message service at the end of the ritual.[28]

The remarkable by-product of this shared liminality is the resulting communitas:

> The membership in the Unity Science Church consists of community members from diverse ethnic and racial backgrounds. Economically, the believers belong to the lower socioeconomic levels of society. . . . Most church members have common feelings of despair . . . as a result of rapid change in the sociopolitical and economic structures of the city brought by rapid urbanization, resulting in alienation from family, friends, and previous group affiliations.[29]

These involuntarily liminal ones are rendered as such by their culture, and yet they find meaning through voluntary participation in liminal religious experience. The sacred dimension encountered through the ritual trance is experienced collectively:

> This is accomplished by taking all members of the church into a liminal state during the church service. . . . It is through the church service that the group is collectively taken from its usual cultural conditions into a state of symbolic suspension, a liminal state, during which time the believers experience a merging of earth and spiritual planes.[30]

This sub-culture preserves a definite role for ritual and trance states within a specified religio-mythical boundary, and as such, the liminal state is revelatory, full of personal and collective transforming power.

# Chapter 5
# In Our Stars or in Our Genes

In our contemporary context, research in the areas of both the biogenetic and psychotherapeutic have found a new engagement with and redefinition of liminal states of being. The continuing conversation between scientific, medical, and psychological paradigms of the person and society both challenge and confirm traditional, cultural, mythic, or religious understandings. The distinctive languages of differing anthropologies often start with different questions and conclude with different answers, but all find continuing fascination with and helpfulness from renewed examination of the latent and actual power which is found only at that liminal threshold.

Researchers with a structuralist and biogenetic orientation have continued to search for principles which underlie human ritual. As such, they view phenomena at the observable level being manifestations of underlying structures which operate from beneath and transform patterns at the surface.[1] Though recognizing non-biological causes, their focus is primarily upon the biological and neurophysiological. In biogenetic influences, behavior is understood to be determined by brain function, brain structure, and genetics, all of which interact with the environment.

In this context, ritual behavior is described as highly structured, repetitive in its occurrence over long periods of time,[2] fostering social interaction through the neuro-motor function of participants.[3] As behavior which is largely biologically determined, "Ritual connotes for both biologists and anthropologists behavior that is formally organized into repeatable patterns."[4]

Because of the pervasive influence of neurobiology on behavior, Barbara Lex observes that ritual trance, so ubiquitous and found in so many forms, "arises from manipulation of universal neurophysiological structures. . . ."[5] The universality of these experiences indicates a biological structural substrate.[6]

This analysis of Lex and other structural biogenetic researchers has been directly applied to rituals common to the rites of passage. Rituals which include rhythmic stimuli of certain kinds produce trance states integral to the liminal state: "Repetitive, evocative sequences of behavior in the separation, transition, and reincorporation phases of rites of passage and rites of intensification establish similar emotional states in participants, restoring individual and group equilibrium."[7]

Turner's concept of communitas, then, is based on shared emotional states, induced by common rituals, connected directly to neurobiological structures.[8] The ambivalence of the liminal state of being is "created by an oscillation between opposing emotional states."[9] This oscillation between emotional states is amplified by the contrast between the figure-ground perception of individual and collective experience. The deliberate goal in the rites of passage of "change in neurophysiological functioning."[10]

Turner's response to what some have called the reductionistic analysis of the neurophysiological approach, was to consider sources for human behavior beyond social conditioning. He enlarged his thinking to include the insights of genetics, neurology, and neurobiology of the brain. He gave special consideration to the work of Paul MacLean, the neuroanatomist, and his theory of the three-layered and developed brain, each aspect having its own phylogenetic history and distinctive organization. Each has its own special intelligence and its own sense of time and space, though interlinked and connected one with the other:

*The Reptilian brain*—the brain stem—responsible for instinctive behavior, fixed action patterns, and innate releasing mechanisms.

*The Paleo-mammalian brain*—the midbrain; the limbic system, including the hypothalamus and the pituitary gland—responsible for homeostatic mechanisms.

*The Neo-mammalian brain*—neocortex, or outer layer of brain tissue; that part of the cerebrum rich in nerve-cell bodies and synapses—responsible for complex mental functions, cognition, sophisticated perceptual processes.[11]

Turner queries how ritualization might have biogenetic foundations:

Can cosmologies, theologies, rituals, meditative techniques, pilgrimages, be the result of either dominant right-hemisphere or left-hemisphere functioning? How does this fit with the varieties of religious experience observed and reported by William James and his school?[12]

Though conceding that deep neurobiological structures most likely do shape much of our individual and collective consciousness, Turner in no way subscribed to a biological reductionism. He reminds his biogenetic structural friends, also on the basis of brain functioning, that the upper brain is quite adaptable; there is a place for both social influence and genetic influence on the ritual process. Accordingly, ritual is still much more than "brain functioning writ large."[13] Most surely it plays a crucial role, but so does the fact that "not one mind, but many minds come together to create and discover realities common to them all."[14] This observation is key, for to explain by one method is not to limit other explanations. For instance, to empirically explain anything in the known universe is not to negate claims of transcendence, because such claims belong to an additional or alternative order of knowing. Many forms of reductionism do not posit such realities, and should not be expected to do so. But neither should one assume that because something has been explained through scientific, sociological, or psychological categories the religious claim has been eliminated. It is a separate claim of a different kind.

From their epistomological point of view, Eugene d'Aquili and Andrew Newberg have insisted that whatever liminal threshold states are traversed between various levels of social hierarchy in the rites of passage, their etiology still remains underlying neuropsychological states and structures. As ceremonial ritual is the most frequently practiced psychosocial agency during such times, it remains the unifying key through which the social, neuropsychological, and mythic dimensions are demonstrated and integrated. The affective results of ceremonial ritual are pan-religious; as a morally neutral act, ritual depends upon mythic and cultural meanings to determine its result.[15] The ambiguity of liminal states is joined by the shared experience of the unitary state of ritual to create a sense of communitas.[16]

The intra-psychic states which are produced during ceremonial ritual often share common characteristics with the unitary states generated by various meditative practices, because the same underlying neurological functions are involved. As in types of meditation, the form and type of ritual informs the resulting affect by the ways in which it stimulates the brain and nervous system. "Slow rhythmicity seems to drive the trophotropic system to ever increasing intensity, while rapid rhythmicity seems to drive the ergotropic system to ever increasing intensity."[17] It only follows that different forms of ritual piety actually stimulate different neuropsychological mechanisms.

When reduced to the level of the neurophysiological, experience of the sacred, beauty, a sense of mystery, and the most moving human experiences all become aspects of biological function, with the brain as perceptual machine. In this sense, all reality, as it is known, is either perceived or generated by the brain.[18]

Though it is important to recognize that the brain and central nervous system is the primary agency through which all such experience is mediated and experienced, a radical biological reductionism does not address larger epistemological questions. Is mind equivalent to the material status of the brain, or does mind precede or transcend brain? Is reality limited to a subjective perception of it? Does this mean one perception or the collective perceptions of many? Does this hold true throughout time and many cultures? And are the neurophysiological states beneath the socio-mythic liminal phase of the rites of passage the genesis of the ritual, or the result? Or both? Such questions cannot be completely answered from within the Biogenetic model, for they stand both inside and outside of its frame of perception.

# Chapter 6
# Continuity and Context

If scientific enquiry into the biogenetic structural dimensions of liminal reality locates a neuropsychological etiology beneath mythic and social passage, a changing cultural context finds traditional forms of rites of passage and the liminal state of being also redefined. Recent comparative studies in liminality have identified the ways in which contemporary culture creates equivalents to pre-modern liminal forms.

As Turner's work provided theoretical foundations for the reformulation of many problems in divergent disciplines, there emerged broadening study of comparative liminality. The most intentional effort at inter-disciplinary study of liminality was the ongoing *Jerusalem Seminar on Comparative Liminality,* which was held for many years at the Hebrew University of Jerusalem under the direction of S.N. Eisenstadt and Victor Turner.

With special attention to studies of both ritual and non-ritual liminality, Turner drew a distinction between the ritual liminality of pre-industrial societies and the non-ritual liminality of post-industrial societies with his coined expression, the *liminoid.* Liminoid states are those removed from the pre-modern schema of the rites of passage while maintaining a "betwixt and between" sense of set-apart reality. The liminoid experiences in industrial, now technological, modern societies represent a persistence of the tribal and classical liminality though removed from their traditional contexts and having become highly individualized.

Does something similar to this culturally constructed or contractile liminal space-time exist at all in Leviathan or Megalopolis, in large-scale, complex, industrial societies, with a fine-cut division of labor, developed class structure, plural ethnicities, manifold voluntary associations, fast and elaborate means of communication and transportation, linked to an international economy, and monitored and reflected by multiple electronic media? Indeed, can one speak of transitions, limina, at all, when everything appears to be in continuous transition, in everlasting flux?[1]

Is there a need to generate limina, some sense of timelessness in in the midst of time? What contemporary agencies provide an analogous function? Do they perhaps tap into some of the same deep structures beneath the surface, if not into the same pre-industrial ritual forms? And how are traditional liminal states—which predominate in tribal, early agrarian and collective societies and share a common mythos—similar to, yet different from new and emerging liminoid forms?

Among many modern people, there is a clamoring for the liminoid with a simultaneous rejection of the liminal as it is found in traditional religious or ritualized form. For those in a very individualistic society which treasures choice and not obligation, the liminoid is somehow felt to be freer than the liminal: "One works at the liminal, one plays with the liminoid."[2] In the rejection of the mythos or world view which provides ritual form and interpretation of the affective states accompanying the liminal, there remains today "what one might call a growing need for liminoid spaces and times."[3] People seek altered affective states, often through non-religious or non-mythical rituals.

The most graphic and culturally accessible example is that of contemporary media and the ways in which it creates liminoid states and resulting, however artificial, communitas. Elihu Katz and Daniel Dayan presented an analysis of the media and its fabrication of liminoid experience in yet another paper of the Jerusalem Seminar.[4]

Viewing television is an activity in which masses of people regularly disconnect themselves from everyday reality and "allow themselves to be transported symbolically elsewhere."[5] Within this type of liminoid activity there is a genre of live broadcasts of great events that transform individuals and separated social groups "into the communitas of whole societies."[6] Preplanned ceremonial occasions of great import such as the funeral of JFK, the coming of Sadat to Jerusalem, the Royal Wedding, and even the bombing of Baghdad in the Persian Gulf War draw in the viewer as observer vicariously participating in the larger than life narrative and ceremonial ritual. Through the media, most citizens, everywhere at once, have access to the great contests, conquests, and coronations which bind them together in a communitas of common observation and vicarious participation. In the heightened and dramatized moment of airing, presentations provide introduction and resolution, reminders of historical importance and an air of reverence which is larger than and apart from the mundane aspects of day-to-day existence.[7] Thus the omnipresence of televisions in the day rooms of nursing homes, a liminoid solution for the involuntary liminality of old age.

Modern forms of tourism serve as liminoid forms of ancient, and sometimes still practiced, liminal rites of pilgrimage.[8] Thus the rise of "get-away" vacations. But get away from what, to what, and with what purpose?

When Geoffrey Chaucer wrote his *The Canterbury Tales* it was a fanciful tale of thirty pilgrims beginning their journey at the Tabard Inn in Southwark and proceeding toward its conclusion at Canterbury. Standing in the background of this particular narrative, though, is much of the history of actual medieval pilgrimages. As physical journeys, the pilgrimages required no little effort, planning, and sacrifice. Spiritual in its intent, the journey was a metaphorical action embodying the way of life toward God.[9] As in other religious pilgrimages, the time and effort of travel was long and arduous. Geographic boundaries were crossed, the identity of the traveler and stranger assumed, and forms of mortification accepted, including but not limited to fastings, physical hardship, prolonged pietistic postures, and prescribed prayers. All of these were seen to be normative aspects of the pilgrimage. By intent pilgrims undergo a separation from ongoing life and social status and pass into a condition for which none of their previous experience has prepared them. The pilgrims surrender former social position as they join with others in assuming anonymous identity.[10] In the pilgrimage, the liminal is framed by the initial separation of departure and the venerated object of arrival. In Chaucer, the beginning point of the Inn and destination of the Cathedral contain double metaphorical layers, metaphors for the world and the heavenly realm, respectively. The two sites are separated by more than geography—namely, the symbolic distance between the profane and the sacred. This duality is mediated by means of a transitional journey. Communitas is created through the egalitarian relationships found within the rituals of reversal, particularly as the socially inferior aspire to symbolic superiority and the socially superior aspire to symbolic humiliation.[11]

In contrast to the liminal character of pilgrimage, modern tourism seeks comfort, avoidance of suffering, convenient and fast travel, and accentuated status to which one is already accustomed. This precludes meditation on the interim state and the mediation of dynamic polarities. Though it provides a type of escape to "another world," it is one most usually viewed from behind the safety glass of first-world amenities and luxury class accommodations. On a superficial level, this liminoid form has some parallels with the liminal. One does travel, change location, and partially leave home. Most conspicuously absent, though, is entry into sacred time and space in which one genuinely participates in a rite of passage. Travelers in this liminoid form of pilgrimage lack transformation and wonder why nothing has actually happened.

Indeed, the new and electronically created artificial world of "cyberspace" is a liminoid presentation of realities, relationships, and information previously provided by direct imagination and social interaction. Participants enter into this world behind the screen *believing* in its reality; it is as real as the world in front of the screen. The passageways, locales, time or absence and suspension of time, lead to alternative reality, a virtually created world. To turn on the computer is to become a liminoid creature, assuming new status, leaving behind constraints, and playing by new or revised rules. Except for the economically determined access or inaccessibility to the technology, it makes available a radical egalitarianism with others sharing in the same virtual reality.

The modern communications revolution is capable, say some, of creating "virtual tribes" or "electronic tribes." As *Megatrends* futurist John Naisbitt writes in a more recent book:

> E-mail is a tribe-maker. Electronics makes us more tribal at the same time it globalizes us. From particle physicists to accountants, associations of professionals take on symbolic and tribal-like rituals.[12]

Such a use of technology surely engenders a virtual liminoid reality and virtual forms of artificial communitas.

If there is a flight from the traditional liminal to the contemporary liminoid, what are the impulses and the deep structures which lie beneath the drive toward it? And why, as many members of modern societies flee from constraining rituals, do they simultaneously find themselves either in search of and returning to ancient forms or creating new ones? The modern person, though perhaps rejecting religious understandings of truth and institutional forms of expressing and living faith, nevertheless still seeks transcendence, metamorphosis, and a reality beyond the flat, one-dimensional, disenchanted one in which they live. A misguided quest for this transcendence often leads them out of the emptiness to objects, relationships, compulsive behaviors, and addictions which only amplify the absence of that for which they really long. In times of personal and communal crisis, this drive and need is only heightened.

In her study of ritual activity at Rachel's Tomb in Bethlehem during the 1940's, Susan Sered argues that there is a direct correlation between the rise of and return to ritual action as whole societies find themselves in transitional times:

> A process of ritual revitalization took place at Rachel's Tomb in Bethlehem. . . . I argue that during the 1940's, the Jewish community in Palestine was, collectively, in a state of 'societal liminality'.[13]

In such times, an increase in pilgrimages to shrines of saints can be seen as an attempt to make sense out of current reality by "linking it to sacred history."[14] Many and various factors may cause dormant symbols to re-emerge, or new symbols to be born. When rumors and news of the Holocaust in Europe began to reach Palestine, and continued as survivors of the death camps began to arrive, a vast array of ritual practice and behavior proliferated around Rachel's tomb. These decades were in fact a time between the times for the majority of the Jewish population in Palestine, a period of social liminality; one which was, in many respects, expressed and interpreted through symbolic ritual.

# Chapter 7
# Present-Day Passage

Perhaps nowhere has the modern liminoid equivalent to pre-modern liminality been more in evidence than in the various psychotherapeutic practices of this century. When Levi-Strauss equated psychoanalysis with older, traditional ritual cures, he described the present-day psychoanalyst as a modern shaman. This modern shaman has much to benefit by "comparing its methods and goals with those of its precursors."[1] If treatments have become conversions, the language of symbols, particularly ritual action, is most efficacious.[2] One such learning from our psychoanalytic ancestors would be that psychic contents appearing in the patient's subconscious are mythic in form and transcend the personal experience and memory of the patient.[3] In this thinking, the unconscious ceases to be a repository of only unique and individual peculiarities; it contains broader, deeper contents.[4]

By citing important parallels and places of informative contact between what Turner would call the earlier liminal and post-industrial liminoid, Levi-Strauss brings forth the universal aspects of both. In fact, he goes so far as to claim that the logic of mythical thought is not only as rigorous as that of modern science, but makes the debatable observation that the "same logical processes operate in myth as in science."[5] He moderates a view of a universe full of rational universals with some exceptions, one being that "in industrial civilization there is no longer any room for mythical time, except within."[6] The identified commonalities still dwarf particularities and there is in his thinking little tension between what are understood to be ancient and modern forms of the same reality.

Don Browning makes the same kind of observation as he relates the relevance of Turner's thought to the modern psychologies, especially those of the humanistic variety.

> Modern therapies too are marked by a moment of separation in which a patient's former socializations, introjections, and community loyalties are looked at, reflected upon, examined, and quite likely brought into question, either in part or as a whole. Then there may be a period of

28

liminality, by which Turner means a period of betwixt and between, when the client is neither completely content with his or her old values nor has replaced them with new ones. The final phases of therapy may be a time of reaggregation during which the client re-establishes what Jerome Frank calls a new 'assumptive world'—a new belief and value framework which usually creatively combines aspects of old values with new ones that have been more autonomously chosen.[7]

Though not mentioning the finer distinctions between the liminal and the liminoid, Browning recognizes a fundamental difference between the pre-modern and modern forms of this reality:

Obviously, as Turner would be quick to point out, in more primitive societies the moment of reaggregation involves a deeper and more internalized acceptance of a set of values and beliefs which have been predetermined by the society.[8]

Jan and Murray Stein, for instance, claim that psychotherapy is the contemporary instrumentality of transition which in large part replaces earlier ritual patterns of passage.[9] As an equivalent system, psychotherapy provides counterparts to separation, liminality, and reintegration. In psychotherapeutic terms the correspondences are psychological destructuring, flux and turmoil, and restructuring.

Recognizing liminal parallels and noting that psychotherapy is a present-day creation of ancient initiation rituals, but missing the important distinctions between the liminal and liminoid, they observe:

To us, liminality seems to be the heart of the mid-life transition and the key to understanding its nature and psychological function . . . it is legitimate to speak of mid-life liminality as potentially transformative. . . . In the midst of the emotional flux and turmoil of midlife liminality, persons struggle with fundamental splits and dynamics of their personalities and undergo internal structural changes that will affect their attitudes and emotional reactions permanently. The net result will be a transformation of consciousness.[10]

Indeed, liminal categories of thought have been used psychotherapeutically to interpret the meaning of depression in important transitional moments. As a liminal quality, death experiences of the self frequently translate into depression, a catalyst for forms of rebirth.[11]

Though many theorists and practitioners miss this distinction between the liminal and the liminoid, there are those who have moved beyond a simple appropriation of Turner's liminal categories. They have brought a more self-conscious critical evaluation of and reflection on the distinctions between the liminal and the liminoid in contemporary psychotherapy.

Robert Moore is a proponent of appropriating liminal categories of thought to serve as a model for transformation in psychotherapy. After careful examination, Moore came to discover that most if not all therapies contain highly ritualized and formalized elements. Most important for him was the insight that psychopathology and psychotherapy might best be understood from an anthropological perspective.

> Instead of viewing rituals of healing and systems of personal transformation in religious traditions as primitive psychotherapy, one could just as easily view contemporary psychotherapeutic practices as expressions of ritual process which offer a small segment of our population a source of ritual leadership in times of crisis.[12]

The small group therapy movement is a remarkable example of the role of a ritual leader, a set-apart liminoid community in time and space which creates a sense, however artificial, of communitas. Some practices of these movements utilized what could only be described as ceremonial ritual elements such as sensory stimulants.[13] Moore summarizes:

> The special forms of ritually created psychosocial space-time offer a place where the individual can experiment with new images of both self and others and with new behavioral modalities which the world of structure may require. These new thoughts, feelings, and behaviors may be enacted in various ways within the secured boundaries of the therapeutic container and worked through until the individual is prepared to attempt a reassertion of his or her autonomy and a return to ordinary life.[14]

In contrast to Moore, Volney Gay presents a scathing portrait of psychotherapy created by and participating in the cultural breakdown which it presumes it can repair. For Gay, contemporary psychotherapy becomes a prime example of an artificially created liminoid form. Liminoid constructions, in this way of thinking, are not only weak substitutes for truly liminal dimensions of passage and genuine forms of communitas; as fabrications, they are the products of the breakdown of liminal communitas. Psychoanalysis has simply developed in tandem with this disintegration, and rather than addressing the origins of the dysfunction, has become a colluding partner with it.

> Both narcissism and its psychoanalytic treatment are liminoid. Psychoanalysts, psychoanalytic theory, and psychoanalytic treatment are restrictive, individual, arranged in schools, potentially revolutionary, ritualized but not religious, and shaped by the commodity dimension of our culture. More importantly, the problems with which psychoanalysis is designed to deal are, in part, products of the dissolution of liminal communitas.[15]

In a fractured world, divided into distinct arenas and social strata, psychoanalysis contributes to the fracturing as it is immensely private, selective and arcane in its action.[16] The privatization of life, reinforced by psychoanalysis, only tears down authentic communitas as it simultaneously elevates the liminoid. As narcissistic pathologies have direct bearing on powerful shifts in family and social life, discussions of liminal and liminoid forms of life and therapy become increasingly important.

Moore's strength is found in the identification of the deep structural human need for both liminal-like forms of passage and a resulting communitas. The positive contribution of Gay is found in his siren warning directed toward therapies which may be oblivious to the relationship of individual to culture and the ways in which they have been co-opted and sometimes created by their own context. Though Gay's characterizations of certain therapists may be accurate, one does have the feeling he is in conversation with a psychoanalytic straw figure from the past. Therapy as a whole is more integrative and holistic today, with family systems approaches being just one example of a recognized larger context in which the individual exists. In his overgeneralizing, one must wonder at what he proposes. A return to the liminality which Turner observes in village-based, agrarian, life-cycle oriented, pre-industrialized cultures? If so, just how would such a return take place? And if not a return, which seems little less than impossible, then what? Is it not feasible, on the other hand, to speak of identifying the dynamics which are at work in pre-modern liminal experience and find equivalents which function in a new but unique context?

Moore believed it was. In an attempt to find reasonable equivalents and apply them therapeutically, he reconceptualized Turner's definitions of the liminal and liminoid. Whereas Turner made distinctions primarily in terms of social location—pre-modern ritualized passage vs. industrialized non-ritual or non-religiously oriented states of being—Moore draws the distinctions quite differently. For Moore, the primary boundary is rather framed in terms of the presence or absence of ritual leadership and transformative space.

> While liminal space requires ritual leadership, liminoid space does not. A ritual leader may be present in liminoid space, but must be present for liminal space to exist. Liminality can occur at or near the center in tribal society not just because the social processes are relatively "simple," integrated, or totalistic but because of the availability of knowledgeable ritual elders who understand how transformative space is located, consecrated, and stewarded.[17]

It is liminal space which is set by the clearly prescribed boundaries of sacred territory and space. Liminoid realities may be positioned on the edge of structure, with free-floating but undefined sensation, but they lack the power to foster transition. Such a defined and boundaried therapeutic space has come to be understood by current Freudian and Jungian analysis as the essential transforming container in which the process must take place.[18] Clarification is indeed necessary in understanding the distinctiveness of the liminal and liminoid, but the key to that understanding is in the presence or absence of authentic ritual leadership in transformative space.[19]

# Chapter 8
# More than Madness

The American Psychiatric Association has defined Brief Psychotic Disorder as a disturbance lasting more than one day and remitting by one month.[1] Symptoms include disorganized thinking and behavior, catatonic motor behaviors, morbidity, affective flattening, alogia, and avolition.[2] Extensive research which relies upon current scientific models has been conducted into the etiology of psychotic disorders. Depending upon which schools of thought are queried, the sources of the defined disorders may include genetics, biochemistry, physiology, psychology, sociology, and family dynamics.[3]

Dissociative disorders, which are not to be confused with brief psychotic disorders, contain a disruption in the usual flow and function of consciousness. Dissociative disorder especially affects memory, identity, and perception, and may be sudden or gradual, transient or chronic. Frequently coupled with dissociation is amnesia, the sudden and unexpected travel referred to as fugue, confusion of identity and a deep sense of depersonalization.[4] Not all dissociative states are to be considered pathological, however. Dissociative states are a common and expected aspect of religious life in many cultures and sub-cultures.[5] Trance states entered into voluntarily and as the result of religious ritual should not be confused with the hallucinations and delusions of a psychosis, and are distinguished by their congruency with their own culture and relative brevity.[6]

As we recognize the important contributions of current scientific schools of thought to the understanding and treating of that which has come to be labeled a brief psychotic episode, we must also recognize the relative nature of those claims. All systems of knowing are constructed with inevitable presuppositions of reality, ways of construing the world which often eclipse other ways of perception. Indeed, "Science has now become widely thought to be not the way one understands the world but merely one possible interpretation of a certain aspect of collective human experience."[7] There is no such thing as pure and absolute objectivity in seeing, recording, and drawing conclusions. And yet once a scientific paradigm is established as normative, the paradigm not only gains universal acceptance, but often comes to be defended in spite of evidence to the contrary—a pursuit of the most dogmatic kind.[8] The harshest critique of the forms of science which foster the most reductionistic, empirical view of the world, is that they create a mechanistic and instrumental perception of the world which is internalized by members of its culture. Its objectification of the world not only leads to an objectification of persons and nature, but to the lack of a participating consciousness between self and world. Inevitably, subjects also become objects.

> Scientific consciousness is alienated consciousness: there is no ecstatic merger with nature, but rather total separation from it. Subject and object are always seen in opposition to each part of the world around me. The logical end point of this world view is a feeling of total reification: everything is an object, alien, not-me; and I am ultimately an object too, an alienated 'thing' in a world of other, equally meaningless things. This world is not of my own making; the cosmos cares nothing for me, and I do not really feel a sense of belonging to it. What I feel, in fact, is a sickness in the soul.[9]

If we were to see the brief psychotic episode from an alternate view of reality, outside of the scientific consciousness, we would understand, describe, and interpret what these episodes mean quite differently. Indeed, in many primitive cultures, what we have called the brief psychotic episode (as opposed to life-long, debilitating, harmful, or dangerous manifestations) is not only tolerated but venerated as a means to a deeper and expanded consciousness, including divine dimensions and a new place in the tribal or social order.[10] In our Western culture, such human phenomena represent a threat to the structure and order of rational life; there is no room for such persons. The frequent result is a response opposite that of the so-called primitive society; we increase suffering as we isolate and ostracize.

The Rites of Passage model is a helpful alternative interpretive model for both understanding and facilitating movement through these profound interpersonal and intra-psychic transitions. Such a model of transition is dynamic and requires an alternate anthropology and ontology. One of the best ways to understand the betwixt and between character of this liminal state is through the study of psychotic episodes and cross-cultural anthropology.

When the IXth International Congress of Anthropological and Ethnological Sciences took up the theme of Anthropology and its relationship to Mental Health, the topic of psychotic episodes played no small part. In an effort to examine mental health from an expanded point of view, the congress intentionally assembled a cross-cultural array of anthropologists.[11] One of the remarkable presentations of the Congress dealt with graphic expression by persons experiencing psychotic episodes in New Guinea.[12] An important facet of this research was the comparison of the graphic expression of both Western and New Guinea patients during parallel stages of psychotic episodes. Though the meaning and treatment of psychotic episodes differs in the two cultures, patterns of graphic expression have striking similarity in structure and form.

Research begins with study of the non-psychotic art of each culture. Such familiarity is necessary as a beginning point from which to make distinctions. Though each culture provides a distinctive artistic form for graphic expression, acutely regressed patients of both cultures come to produce structures with much greater similarity. These representations correspond to levels of disintegration and personality organization and include simple inarticulate shapes, two-dimensionality, and mere scribblings. Representations of the natural environment become hyper-geometric. There emerges a prevalence of mandala-like designs. This is true of graphic expression during psychotic episodes in both cultures."[13]

The more the person with a psychosis separates into a state of separated liminal reality, the less cultural form and particularity influences expression, and the more primary, universally held images predominate. If this movement from individual memory and cultural particularity to collective and transcultural universal symbol reflects a phylogenetic reality, it may mean the accessing of the older tripartite brain. In terms of consciousness and its metaphors, this leads us to a discussion of individual ego consciousness, the primary thought of unconsciousness, and the relationship to a collective or transpersonal consciousness.

It is not uncommon for psychiatrists and psychoanalysts to explain the formation of an individual's intra-psychic images primarily as the product of memory traces which assume the form of representations. Affect is attached to the image and is recalled when the image is recalled, a substitute for the actual external object. This imagery not only interprets reality but serves as a surrogate for it. And the recording of perception is primarily the function of the more recent and complex cerebral cortex of the brain.

Though these theorists and practitioners draw clear and convincing conclusions relating to personal images, memory, and unconscious; and though they recognize the different orders of emotions, from instinctual emotions to second-order emotions related to remembered images; no place is reserved for that which might transcend the personal. The only explanation for primitive paleosymbols is that one returns to private meanings known only to their beholder.[14] This kind of idiosyncratic explanation is not adequate. It does not go far enough because it is incapable of seeing more than it expects to see due to the limits of its perceptual model. It cannot see or take into account an alternative view of such phenomena as might be indicated in the cross-cultural research from the graphic expression of those passing through psychotic episodes. It is quite possible to understand the disorganization which takes place in brief psychotic episodes, as well as dissociative states, ritual trance, and mystical experience *alternatively*, as passage into an intra-psychic liminal state which holds symbols of a universal nature extending beyond or beneath personal unconscious.

Though Carl Jung recognized the operation of a personal unconscious and memory which retains experience and affect affiliated with it, his phenomenological method located a source and etiology beyond personal experience alone, which was expressed in image and symbol:

> The fact is that certain ideas exist almost everywhere and at all times, and they can spontaneously create themselves quite apart from migration and tradition. They are not made by the individual, but rather they happen; they even force themselves upon the individual's consciousness.[15]

The origins of universal image and symbol originate in the transpersonal:

> Even dreams are made of collective material to a very high degree, just as in the mythology and folklore of different peoples, certain motives repeat themselves in almost identical forms. I have called these motives "archetypes" and by them I understand forms or images of a collective nature which occur practically all over the earth as constituents of myths and at the same time . . . individual products of unconscious origin.[16]

The intra-psychic liminal plunge into the anti-structure of that state is not simply a separation from ego consciousness, nor merely an entry into the personal subconscious; it is entry into a collective, transpersonal consciousness. It is not surprising that many pre-moderns passing through liminal transition, especially that which is characterized by ecstatic, non-rational states, found that which was revelatory, sacred, and the source of special wisdom and knowledge. So it has been for the mystics and adherents of ecstatic religious experience throughout time.

Strong parallels exist between the process of the brief psychotic episode and the mythical stories of transition and transformation, especially those of initiation in the rites of passage. There is often a common pattern: a period of separation from not only social order but also from the structure of the ego; a retreat inward and backward in time to an undifferentiated and liminal state deep in the psyche; and, finally, a reaggregation into a new and transformed life.

In John Perry's understanding of and approach to brief psychotic episodes, he has attempted to interpret them as legitimate, though entirely nonrational, and alternate states of being.[17] The symbolic subjective content with which a person becomes engrossed during acute schizophrenia is understood to be meaningful, and not merely random disorder. Medication may only repress the emergence of such images and symbols, which are themselves keys to a whole new phenomenology of the psychosis.[18] Perry presents the argument that brief psychotic episodes often contain healing potential capable of reorganizing the deep, common patterns of the psyche. Having a life and pace of its own, the process of transformation is best served by serious attention given to the resulting symbols and images.[19] The pattern of emerging imagery from the psyche is one of dissolution and reconstruction,[20] parallel to the classical outline of renewal found in ancient myth and ritual ceremony.[21] What may seem senseless or irrational to the unaware observer actually makes perfect sense when related to the narrative lines of the great mythological journeys. These narratives emerge as the mirror images of deep inward peregrinations of the psyche. In relating the predictable aspects of the inner journeys of many individuals passing through acute psychotic episodes to the repeating themes of passage and transition found in the great mythologies, Perry identifies the following:

1. Establishing of a world center as the locus
2. Passage through death
3. Return to the beginnings of time and the creation
4. Cosmic conflict as clash of opposites
5. Threat of reversal of opposites
6. Apotheosis as king or messianic hero
7. Sacred marriage as union of opposites
8. New birth as reconciliation of opposites
9. New society of prophetic vision
10. Quadrated world forms[22]

Since defining madness is a socially driven behavior, Perry exposes just how the practice of labeling becomes "a component incorporated into the psychotic process, and built into its structure, determining its progress and outcome."[23] During the psychotic episode, the vulnerable ego not only identifies with its subconscious contents but also with external cultural and social identifications, taking the identity upon itself.

A truly helpful therapeutic methodology should be guided by the healing potential of the powerful narrative and symbolic images and their accompanying emotions. Such images manifest the descent by the transitional person into identification with the archetypal and underlying structures and their seeming timelessness.[24] As opposed to traditional therapeutic approaches which only view such phenomena as symptoms in the service of reality avoidance, a loss of object relations, and the withdrawl of cathexes and its resulting regression, Perry suggests a healing posture which embraces the symbolic language of the rich and powerful affective images. A correlate to such serious consideration of the psychic phenomena is the unorthodox proposal that the process should be allowed to run its course without electro/chemical intervention; in fact, such intervention may undermine the integrity of the psyche's healing transition. In the same way that sedatives given at the time of grief may repress the very emotional functions which are painfully prerequisite to healing, so the administration of medications may in fact hinder, if not prohibit, the intra-psychic passage. As such, therapy requires a guide willing to traverse liminal terrain on its own terms. As found in the ritual-dramas of transformation in world mythology, the liminal personae must pass through the liminal phase between separation and reaggregation, through disintegration into reintegration.

In exploring an existentialist perspective on brief psychotic episodes, Francis Macnab has drawn upon the work of Martin Heidegger, Martin Buber and Paul Tillich.[25] Seriously considering the various etiologies emerging from different schools of thought, including biochemically-based causes, Macnab describes the psychotic episode as one of psychic non-being, estrangement, separation from a determining center, the loss of courage, and the inability to decide. Separated from relationship to a center, removed from meaningful being-in-the-world and foundational securities, the person regresses into, or progresses toward, a confusing and ambiguous state of liminal non-being.[26] The liminal person in radical separation, in miscarried attempts to make something of the self-world relation, falls into an extreme state of estrangement wherein both the self and his world suffer tremendous upheavals.[27]

In this view, the way to healing is relational; one seeks connection to the deep self by means of its own symbol and language system. The self provides the means by which reconciliation may take place, not only with inner core realities, but also with place-in-the-world and being-with-others in the world. Beyond tragic estrangement, the liminal being is transformed with a new, reaggregated, and transformed center on the other side of psychic disintegration and death. Terrifying vacancy is also terrifying fullness. Estrangement from one *state of being* precipitates passage to *another*. New relationship on the other side of estrangement is the completion of the process and the time of re-embodiment and reaggregation.

As the psyche contains a series of oppositional thresholds which must be encountered and crossed, liminal reality is that state of being located between one dominant self-image and a new identity. This new identity "is known to be different from the persona, is feared to be the shadow, and actually moves, if successful, toward a more comprehensive dominant self-image than the one transiently abandoned in the liminal state."[28] Liminal space and time serve as the locale of movement, a crossing and recrossing, from any established structure of the psyche to another.[29] As the transcendent function unites the conscious and unconscious and various oppositions without destroying them, the "self-image undergoes a more or less marked stage of liminality, betwixt and between."[30]

*Part II*

# Introduction

The religious leader is strategically positioned, both in terms of specific roles within faith communities and also by virtue of a particular theological worldview, to be an extremely important ritual guide to individuals, groups, and social and ecclesial systems upon entrance into liminal states within passages. The pastoral leader may approach liminal reality with unique fields of meaning which are frequently more applicable to liminal reality than those of other schools of thought. Assessment, guidance, and healing based on such categories as awareness of the holy, providence, faith, grace, repentance, communion, and vocation[1] are especially suited to interpreting transitional phenomena and the intrinsic potentials for transformation they hold.

The communitas of shared liminal reality—resulting from brief passage or permanent forms of liminality—is the forming power of all spiritual communities. The ritual leader serves as symbolic mediating presence, standing at thresholds, reminding the community of its identity through the articulation of the guiding symbols, metaphors, and narratives into which it has been initiated. In the midst of these moments of transition, it is possible to encounter the sacred in new and vital ways.

The liminal guide lives fluidly between the world of structure and its antithesis. One's unique position betwixt and between enables new categories of perception: madness and mysticism may be redefined, ecstatic experience renewed to its legitimate place, the relationship between body and mind reconciled, genetics and environmental conditioning freed from a false duplicity.

Though knowing the difference between the deeply communal rites of passage which are so closely tied to culture and the earth, the spiritual leader also knows that contemporary life has not completely erased the human hunger for experience beyond its one-dimensional grind. Realities which are set apart, even those fabricated and artificial, have the potential to transform as long as they include the necessary containment of separated space and ritual leadership.

Even the liminal edges of sanity and insanity hold potential revelatory power. The sea which surges within the shores of consciousness holds its treasure; the liminal guide dares to swim there, taking seriously the contents which lead to deeper healing vitalities beneath the surface.

Much religious awareness brings a unique perspective on the interplay between time and space: the movement of the sacred within and yet transcending history, the cycles of life giving shape to both endings and beginnings, ultimate meanings found both in narratives of primal origins and ultimate conclusions.[2] These theological realities are useful not only in the service of interpretation. They are based on and symbolically express the deep structures found within the liminal states. Even those who dismiss the imposition of a mythic overlay of meanings placed upon liminal states, nevertheless find themselves living and experiencing the same deep structural framework and patterns which mythic systems identify and claim.[3]

As a culturally and religiously multi-lingual guide, the religious leader may translate the realities which underlie experience and its descriptions into understandable metaphors of the contemporary mind. The person who understands the transforming power of liminal reality may provide pastoral leadership in a multiplicity of arenas which are characterized by the patterns of the Rites of Passage.

# *Chapter 9*
# The Liminal Locale of Hospitalization

Hospitalization is a liminal state between health and re-found health or death. It is contained, transitional, and potentially life-changing. The chaplain or religious leader may serve in the powerful role of ritual elder and may share "appropriate symbols and rituals with the patient."[1] Isolated, separated from normal modes of being, facing threat of potential pain or death, the patient is faced with the most significant dimensions of life which relate to the sacred.[2]

> The liminal hospital period is out of time and space, outside ordinary reality, and patients know this. If the chaplain is willing to enter this other dimension with them, he or she may be able to help them experience the sacred.[3]

The Rites of Passage model is especially relevant in cases of protracted and sometimes life-threatening illness. As a state of being which is separated from normal life and capacities, the liminal locale of hospitalization may involve severe physical, psychological, and spiritual trauma. The chaplain or pastor enters the liminal state of suffering with a willingness to pass through what may be a transformative passage.[4] At such times patients are unusually accessible, especially in considering and discussing the most important aspects of life, death, meaning, and God.

This ministry must also include the families of patients. Individual family members may not have the particular illness of the patient, but as every family system is an entirety, the entrance of any part of a family system into a liminal state creates parallel dimensions for the whole. If I discover that my child has contracted a life-threatening illness, or that my brother is HIV positive, or that my spouse suffers from a chronic illness, I have entered a liminal reality which is different from but related to that of my family member.

Especially in the case of psychiatry, hospitalization may represent safe containment. It may become a safe place apart from the conflicts or relational failures of ongoing life. Though the patient has entered liminal time and space full of ambiguity and anxiety, this state is bounded by physical location, clearly identified roles, and rituals of the medical model. Whether this time apart is effectively helpful or not is another question, but if a dynamic view of therapy is taken it may provide an opportunity to re-enter ongoing life in a different kind of way. Dramatic changes in provider systems, severely shortened hospital stays, and shifts to outpatient-based models may mitigate against the effectiveness of containment and its provision for a healing place apart.

One of the failures of the deinstitutionalization movement was the elimination of transitional space. The only liminal space left for many of our mentally ill is on the street. They become homeless for many reasons, not the least of which is that they simply cannot function in the land of structure and all it requires. Even if they remember and are able to obtain the medications they need, there is no guarantee that they will take them appropriately. In addition, there is no psychosocial space in which they may transition from one state of being to another. Involuntarily liminal, they have been cast to the margins by a society that keeps them there.

In any kind of hospitalization, patients often experience a form of emotional regression; one moves from a state of autonomy to dependency. Though that regression varies from personality to personality, and depends upon the severity and type of illness, it is maintained and reinforced by the medical institution through daily ritual routine, patient and staff costuming, and highly structured mini-drama conferences in which patient-professional roles are clarified. This maintaining of dependency is one dimension of medical containment. The liminal space is boundaried, the liminal person takes on the persona of one who is transitional, and authoritative roles of healers are assumed. Within this structured liminal environment, the patient is paradoxically encouraged to submit and to fight, become the object of investigation and procedures, and yet participate and take responsibility for his or her own healing. If recovery and healing is possible, or some sustaining equilibrium achieved, its ultimate effectiveness will be related to the ways in which patients recover their autonomy upon reaggregation into ongoing time and space in their world. This re-entry of the patient into their own social world remains one of the great challenges for health care providers and chaplains of all kinds. Institutions customarily understand their reality from the inside out. They take responsibility for those passing into their liminal world where roles, procedures, and rituals are prescribed, but have relative uneasiness in reaching beyond the safety of their own created boundaries.

The chaplain is one who voluntarily enters liminality with those who are there involuntarily. Identification with the one who suffers does not necessarily come from direct personal experience of the presenting illness or conflict known by the patient. It is impossible to have experienced the identical dilemma of every patient. The chaplain, as one personally initiated into liminal reality on some level or in some way, relates *analogically* with the patient. Personal experience may not have provided direct knowledge of, say, amputation, stroke, or blindness, but few have not experienced significant loss of some kind. In the same way that mystics of large spiritual stature have entered into the liminal worlds of those involuntarily liminal by condition, so the chaplain dares to go to those with whom there may be a communitas of the heart.

Though the role of the institutional chaplain is similar to that of a parish pastor in its essential set-apart identity which is grounded in transcendent reality, it is also unique and distinct. The parish pastor participates in established communities, whereas the chaplain enters artificial ones created for specific purposes. If one serves in the correctional system, there exists a community of permanent, involuntary liminality, and a specific ministry is required. In a general hospital system, the community is involuntary but transient, and chaplains must live with that transience. The nature of those communities, and the kind of liminality they embody, determines the kind of liminality and form of ministry in which the chaplain is constantly involved.

More than the character of the communities within the institution, whether permanent or transient, is the personality of the institution itself. The emotional effect on the chaplain is unique in that he or she goes to the liminal place and leaves it, but the place of work *is always liminal.* This requires much from those who have this form of ministry as their vocation. What does it mean to work most of one's hours in a liminal locale? And what does it mean to regularly move back and forth from it to the world of ordinary time and space? The chaplain may leave at the end of the day, to be sure, but he or she must also return. And that is the difference.

Tribal elders in pre-modern initiatory rites entered liminality periodically, but they left it and had their lives grounded elsewhere. Not everyone could remain on the permanent edges. Only the shaman could, and that was possible only by virtue of unique charisms. Can the chaplain stay on the permanent edges without special charisms to do so? Not everyone is capable of living in those locales, and nor are they meant to do so. And if one derives primary income from chaplaincy, can it really be said that it is *voluntary* liminality? If, under conditions of call or employment, one is really *involuntarily liminal,* what self-understanding is required to minister under those terms?

One of the tremendous dangers of institutional ministry is that of absorbing the atmosphere and pathologies of the reality which is held within the walls. In corrections, one may absorb deviancy or hostility. In a psychiatric setting, psychological pathology may find its way toward one's emotional life. In the general hospital setting, illness may do the same.

Identity becomes crucial for the institutional chaplain. As a counterbalance to a fixed vocational liminality, the chaplain must seek out structure to which he or she may return from liminal anti-structure. Many seek and find this structure in concrete hobbies, ordinary routine, and relationships which are unrelated to ministry. Most surely the failure to find personal identity within a vocational life surrounded by the liminal is the emotional and spiritual root of many inappropriate pastoral relationships and pursuits. They have not established a healthy relationship to the structural world of ongoing time and ordinary space and thereby may be drowning in the liminal. The ordained must embrace, negotiate, and live in both structure and anti-structure. And most importantly, they must come to terms with a special role and ontological reality which is like no other in the world.

# Chapter 10
# Higher Education as Liminal Domain

The religious leader is also called to respond to persons in the liminal states which accompany developmental passages. When young adults enter that strange liminal locale of a college campus, they find themselves "unhoused and in transit, having left the familiar behind, neither able to return to it nor yet with a clear idea of what one was destined for and one's ability to get there."[1] As students are separated from tribe, clan and family, they often struggle with ambiguity and a lack of definition. The responses of students to this social transition are mixed. Some are repelled by the ambiguity of their condition and respond with retreat and a return home; others survive but are not transformed. Still others plunge into and through the liminal condition, exploring, experimenting intellectually and socially, and become new persons. In a time when so many cultural rites of passage for children or youth have been eliminated, leaving them to wander toward adulthood, the ritual setting of the college or university still provides the means by which young people may anticipate, rehearse, and pass through prescribed rituals of transition. It is a form of pilgrimage, and the metaphor of the itinerant stranger takes on enlarged importance.

The role of religious leadership is crucial during the liminal college experience accompanied as it is with its often heightened religious/philosophical search and need for a special communitas. Students may be able to look back at their experience of this time, especially at the ritual leadership provided in this semi-permanent liminality, and recognize critical moments of encounter with the Holy.[2] The spiritual need among students, however clearly or unclearly defined, is deep and many times intense. It is present even in the absence of personal or familial religious tradition or experience. This is evidenced in the way students find themselves creating their own rituals if they lack the ones which have been provided by their religious culture. A deep longing somehow searches for a shape and form through which it might be expressed.

The rites of passage are reflected on several different levels in the college experience. If one views the college years as a whole, they may be understood as a rite of passage from one status as a youth to a new status as an adult. Communitas is fostered by the separated locale and shared experience of those passing through the same time in their lives. As the college student is a liminal being, he or she customarily takes on the dress, mannerisms, and sub-cultural definitions of that identity. As one who experiments with identities, the college student rehearses alternative ways of being human. The identification with the subculture is necessary in establishing a critical evaluative distance from the structure from which they have come and to which they will later return. Leadership through the entire transition may be provided by professors, chaplains, and senior peers.

The semester class may itself be seen in similar terms, as a microcosm of the whole college experience. Each class requires entry into a new, separated world which requires the entertaining of new knowledges. An enlarged teaching vocation considers not only the transmission of information, as important as that is, but also the dynamics of passage. From the beginning of any given class until its completion, students will be changed, sometimes dramatically so. This dynamic view of the teaching process recognizes the potential of the liminal period in which the student feels confused by a cognitive, emotional, or even ontological eruption. They stand at the fulcrum between old ways from which they have departed and new ways which are not yet formed. The combined cognitive dissonance and psychological accessibility of this liminal time only elevates the importance of supportive and guiding leadership. The teacher is not only confronted with the demands of intellectual integrity relating to his or her discipline. There is real ethical urgency as regards the guidance of liminal persons. For instance, one cannot ethically knock down old ways of thinking without offering help toward something new. The practice of deconstructing the world-view and beliefs of students in a cavalier way, considered by some as a kind of intellectual sport or mercy killing, has been more destructive than formerly thought. Though satisfying the ego needs of insensitive teachers, this activity provides no ritual leadership in critical moments of initiation which shape not only the world of ideas but actual lives.

Among many students there is a great interest in what has come to be called "spirituality." This may show itself in a traditional form, but just as often it shows itself in unconventional ways. A spiritual opportunity on campus which is experience-based, open-ended in nature, and integrated with psychological insights has broad appeal. Experiential approaches, rather than purely didactic or content-oriented ones, reach more directly into the developmental needs of the students.

This is the backdrop which stands behind the power of small spiritual life groups on campus. They hold explicit goals for spiritual transformation and community. These groups provide a self-conscious faith community which is set apart from even the structure of the college experience as a whole. In this way, the student is not only distanced from the structure of ongoing life by being at college, but from the institution of college by another entity. It represents a border at the border. This may explain why successful locations of campus life groups are often found in a "home" atmosphere which stresses the "home away from home" connection. Usually this is explicitly distanced from both of the institutions of the academy and the church. The home-like containment provides safety and security, and the separation from dominant social institutions provides freedom. Boundaries are present, though fairly fluid, allowing room for exploration and experimentation with new ideas or identities. Sacred time and space are both identified over and against the other structures of their lives. Ministry within this setting tends to be intense because their lives are passing through an intense time.

In most thriving campus ministries the focus remains on sharing faith experiences. The mutuality of the shared liminal pathway creates communitas. The ritual containment of these groups is part of their effective transforming power. There are often traditions for opening, moving the process, and closing in any given meeting. Ritual leadership is expected and desired, though students do not usually want excessive external control. Leading often takes place best through the self-disclosure of the leader and the safety he or she embodies and communicates.

Some colleges have increasingly engaged in more intentional entrance and exit rituals. This includes more extensive orientations which provide initiation into the ethos of the community and small groups and leaders for ready-made relationships. Graduation rituals have always been popular, but some institutions are attempting to amplify these aspects even more. Some campus ministries have developed even more clearly defined rituals of departure and closure, usually taking place during the spring before graduation. They recognize that exit, departure, and reaggregation are mandatory for growth. One campus ministry has developed a "reading of the names" ceremony which lists everyone who has ever been a part of the campus ministry, including the new graduates.

By its very positional nature, campus ministry has always functioned at liminal boundaries. This is one reason ecumenical campus ministry in particular has represented some threat to the traditional church. Because churches most usually occupy space in dominant cultural structure, they are frequently static and characterized by the fear of change. Students, on the other hand, regularly embrace change as a part of their own development and exploration. The fundamental nature of campus ministry is antistructural and liminal.

It has become quite clear in at least the last decade that campus ministry itself has entered a liminal period. This is a different liminality than it ordinarily occupies and of which we have just spoken. This liminality is found in the passage of church's *mission* of campus ministry into a new state. Campus ministry finds itself in a new liminal period because of a new and changing context. It is constantly interacting with social structure, cultural change, and the position of the church. And there are direct ramifications of these interactions for our time.

Ecumenical campus ministry finds itself in much the same dilemma as the rest of the ecumenical movement. Built on a foundation of denominationally created structures, institutionally formed ecumenism is reeling in direct proportion to that of the bodies which sustain it. In addition, denominationally-based campus ministries must deal with what it means to be entering a post-denominational culture. In all of these cases, their platform on the liminal, anti-structural edge is shifting even as are the structures from which they have positioned themselves.

This liminal period of ferment has appeared to create contradictory developments, at least on the surface of things. For instance, ecumenical campus ministry which is based in denominational affiliations finds itself shrinking not only in funding but in participation. The diminishing ability of denominational bodies to adequately fund these ministries is most pressing, but not necessarily the most difficult challenge. The greater obstacle is the quest by most denominations and congregations within them to retrieve a renewed sense of identity. This leaves ecumenical campus ministry not only unfunded, but abandoned. Denominations continue to call upon campus ministry for demonstrable proof of effective service to justify their existence. Increasingly, it is difficult to provide identity-creating examples in the ecumenical context. One after one, ecumenical campus ministries falter and campus ministers become demoralized.

This is not, however, to say that ministry to students has become less important than before. It only reminds us how shifting social models plunge us into liminal states and how something quite different may emerge within its creative process. For instance, at the same time that denominations and ecumenical campus ministry are in a pattern of retreat and retrenchment, larger, broader, and more global ecumenical ministries with students are expanding and proliferating. The World Student Christian Federation (WSCF), which is composed of all the student Christian movements (SCMs) throughout the world, is growing and gaining vitality. The changing needs have provided a global ecumenical opportunity which can be satisfied in no other way. Students are excited, as are the denominations and individuals who fund them.

On the other end of the campus ministry spectrum, local congregations are re-engaging with campus ministry. The focus is on identifiable local faith communities providing campus ministry and they are doing so with ingenuity and commitment. Treasured ecumenical structures on campus are increasingly lost, and the global paradox we have mentioned earlier has come to campus ministry: the more global we become (and we may easily see that we are through the World Student Christian movement), the more local we act (with an increased need for both congregational and denominational identity). And campus ministry will reaggregate on the other side of this liminal passage as something different from what it was before.

If these dynamics are present in the undergraduate college and university setting, do they not also inform our considerations of theological education? Beyond important academic mastery and the acquisition of ministry skills, the liminality of a seminary passage is one which should include significant spiritual formation. As in the church in general, this formation takes place in the midst of boundaried communitas in the presence of the intentional ritual guidance of faculty and peers. This is a powerful argument for maintaining, as much as possible, a residential community of learning and formation. However real the needs of commuting students, as well as those who live off campus, the experience will simply not have the same initiatory and transformational power without established communitas. It goes without saying that entrance into and departure from this sacred time and space is best marked by high ritual in which one's change in status is clearly marked by both church and seminary.

# Chapter 11
# In Season and Out of Season

In usual circumstances, the homiletician is provided some time and preparation in advance of bringing a word to the church. When an event or occurrence plunges an entire community into a state of crisis, the preacher does not have the luxury of a long, sustained time for reflection. This is situational preaching in the extreme and is characterized by a sense of urgency. An immediate response is required. Because the faith community may be more receptive and accessible than at any other time, the preacher must use caution in what is said. But more importantly, it is a time for courage.[1]

As opposed to counseling models which are individual in nature, the homiletic enterprise is primarily concerned with relating to groups of people. As such it has built-in limits and freedoms. The limits have to do with what can be said on a personal level. Preaching simply cannot address persons with the same particularity as does one-to-one counseling. Its freedom is found in an ability to address universal themes in a way that one-to-one conversations cannot. Therein lies its power and its challenge. Homiletic excellence in times of crisis is found among those leaders who are able to address entire communities in such a way that they touch the experience of the individual at the same time.

In applying rites of passage concepts to preaching in times of crisis, it is best to precede it with a special kind of introduction. The purpose of this introduction is to name the reality which has intruded upon the individual, family, or community. We must name the monster that has taken our lives by siege and trace the outlines of what has brought about this terrible moment. To artfully describe the event which has precipitated the crisis is to objectify and identify it as a common experience of suffering which is shared by all. Such a naming includes all feelings surrounding the event, including those which might appear to run counter to faith. Such identified feelings might include anger, doubt, and despair. There must be no denial, no sugar-coating, no avoidance at this point. To speak of anything less than the poignant truth is to delegitimate not only the words of the preacher, but the integrity of the ritual gathering itself. This beginning point of courageous recognition on behalf of the preacher empowers the faint of heart to name the terrible and unspeakable for themselves. And it serves as the introduction for what shall follow.

Because people are confused, disoriented, and often despairing at such times, it is important for the sermon to travel to familiar continuities. Following the introduction which names the experience, the sermon leads toward the structure of pre-liminal reality. This means that the preacher must draw clear connections to the symbols, narratives, tradition, and historic faith by pulling them into the constricted field of vision. People of faith must recall the foundation upon which they have stood in the past in order that they have enough security to deal with the shifting sands of the present. Calling upon the faith found in pre-liminal structure simply recognizes that there are times when the church must believe for us until we can again believe with the church and for ourselves.

Giving a clear account of the historic faith does not mean that we are too hasty in offering simple theological explanations. This includes all manner of speculations as to the will of God. Simple and quick explanations are often thinly disguised forms of avoidance and denial and often negate the seriousness of the crisis. Instead, the preacher must paint the love that will not let us go in broad strokes, leaving the unexplainable particulars to be addressed later.

The sources for resetting this foundation are many and rich: scripture, historic statements of faith, the Lord's Prayer, the great and beloved hymns of the church. The very setting of worship within the church's sacred space implicitly brings forward this wealth. The symbols of faith, a familiar sanctuary, the historic liturgy, an ordained ministry which brings not only the church's authority but the remembrance of many ministers from the past—all of these rekindle an awareness of the reality and mystery that is the ground of our hope.

If the pre-liminal foundation of faith is clearly represented, then the congregation is more ready to enter into the difficult, but necessary exploration of the liminal reality. They are actually in this reality already, so it is not as unwelcome an incursion as the preacher might fear. With the benefit of a re-established foundation and the ritual leadership of the minister, the congregation may be prepared to journey into the ambiguity and unresolved questions. While we do not want to be too hasty in bringing forth theological propositions earlier in the sermon, neither should we be too tardy. The listener is expecting much, in fact no less than a courageous and honest ritual leader who is willing and able to wrestle with the hard questions. This wrestling on the part of the minister gives courage to the listener to do the same, and though the answers may never be completely satisfactory, a faithful response has been attempted and offered. The very fact that someone was willing to attempt to speak a word from the standpoint of faith is encouragement enough for members of the congregation to begin and continue doing their own theology. If this includes an exploration of theodicy, providence, redemption, or healing, they will perhaps carry these same themes forward in their continuing attempt to make sense of what may seem senseless. They hope for a word of faith which dares to come into the situation, however tragic that situation might be. They are also looking for at least *one handle* to which they may hold and from which they may ask more questions and multiply sources of meaning.

After passing through a time of daring homiletical travel in the liminal, the congregation must come to rest. It must not be left in total ambiguity. After all, the goal is one of *passage*. The reaggregation phase ushers the congregation into the future with renewed hope. Though many questions remain unanswered, and will, the congregation is not in the same place. Though there is some sense of structure, it is not the same structure of the preliminal as experienced before the liminal period. It is *restructure*: continuities which have been reshaped by the liminal passage. It is a continuity of being which has been transformed.

After naming the liminal terrain into which individuals and communities have plunged, it is important to maintain a dialogical movement between structure and anti-structure: a foundation is needed in order to explore what seems to have no foundation. Balancing the need for faith continuities with faith exploration is a delicate enterprise. But to such a task the homiletician is frequently called. This work is not for the fearful, though we may indeed feel so. Courage and hope are required for this journey, and the existence of these qualities in the preacher will shape the kind and quality of transformation which must take place.

# Chapter 12
# Liturgy Betwixt and Between

Worship is best understood as a liminal period set over and against the ongoing structure of life. Crucial to the liminal quality of worship is the communitas which is shared among its participants. Ritual and ceremony have the capability to enhance or create this reality, and communitas is often encoded in symbol systems; and the symbol system often has the power to re-invoke past shared experience.[1]

The assumption that worship must be 'relevant' is often misguided, as it misunderstands what constitutes a liminal state and creates communitas. Its confusion is found in attempts to make worship mimic secular form, and in doing so it loses its distinct power. Frequently, the so called "lack of relevancy" criticism is accompanied by attempts to make worship more instrumental in character, as a means to another end—such as propping up civil religion, promoting a particular political agenda or replicating the culture which it attempts to reach. The contention that liminal reality and its resulting communitas is located in anti-structure mitigates against this compulsion to make all relevant. Worship should be a profound anti-structure experience, by its very nature separated from structure.[2] This does not mean that worship cannot be innovative, creative, or expressed in various forms. It most surely can be, and has been throughout the ages. The mistake is found in attempts to reshape it in the mirror of popular culture so that it becomes palatable to secular tastes. True relevancy in liturgy will be found in the degree to which the liminal reality of worship is *made available* to worshippers.

The remoteness of worship from structure in sacred time and space is precisely what irritates those who long for relevancy. And yet this remoteness, this otherness, is the very setting from which its power is derived. This is the location through which word and sacrament enter. We are compelled to bring transformed selves back to the profane world of structure as part of a dialectical process, but nothing will happen if persons are not first formed in sacred time and space; this will not happen if liminal reality dissolves into the world from which it has separated. Related, yes; made to resemble

55

one another, no.[3] In fact, "purging the liturgy of its archaic symbols can be counter-productive. . . ."[4] If anything, transforming worship must become more different from the world in which people find themselves, meeting them correlationally at the point of need without simply reflecting ordinary reality. Even the most effective forms of contemporary or experimental worship tap into predictable rituals which are meaningful to the worshipping community. These rituals may seem irrelevant to those outside of the liminal community, but essential to those within.

The liminal dimensions of the ritual and liturgical setting provide a locale for sacred time and space in which usual categories of time are suspended. Entering such sacred time allows for intense memory as well collapsing the future into the present. The liminal redefining of time in worship grants the symbols, images, and languages of eschatological vision their greatest power. For instance, the internal evidence of Rev. 1:3 and 1:10 makes it clear that John's Apocalypse was intended for recitation in the ritual setting of Christian worship.[5] The liminal setting of worship enabled the articulation of realities transcending time and space. It was the best and most powerful place to speak of such things.

As in artistic creation and expression, worship requires liminal space and time in which it may unfold. Only in such sacred time and space may one pass beyond the surface of images and symbols. The mystery of passage—whether found in the ecstasy of the soul in search of God or in the surrealistic journey through which art leads—wrests timelessness from temporality and marks off perimeters for encounter.[6]

If a primary goal of worship is transformation of the person and community in the presence of God, the presence of sacred time and space must be shepherded by ritual leadership. Without it worship may easily become liminoid, lacking true communitas. A religious rite in which there is no ritual transformative container is "ceremonial," functioning to reinforce and support existing social structures—most surely a projection of existing social structure onto the religious plane. The ceremonial manifestation is often at work in the gatherings of civil religion in which boundaries are blurred between church and state, or the church and an institution of one kind or another.

In contrast, worship in the liminal setting is shepherded by ritual leadership, contains both the presence and interpretation of power-laden symbols of faith, and provides passage into the new and not a return to the old. A change of status must occur. Old wineskins cannot hold new wine.[7] The ceremonial predominates in much of the worship of the church. This is dangerous in terms of transformation, as worship may simply reinforce structure and prohibit entry into liminal anti-structure.

The worshipping community enters into this liminal reality by means of a pilgrimage. It begins with ritual preparation: washing, special dress, a particular meal, a familiar route to the place of worship. But more importantly, it is a pilgrimage to a particular place of contained sacred space and time which is filled with symbols. The processional leads the congregation into this presence, this container, the room and place where the symbols are kept; the physical symbols themselves; the actual and symbolic gathering of the people; and the most complex symbol, the minister.[8]

In the same way that worship demands the liminal, so the Eucharist exists by the function of its own peculiar liminal nature—a sub-liminal reality within the broader liminal reality of the liturgy. The Table of Christ stands apart from ordinary human structure and historical time as it creates communitas among those who share its dramatic, symbol-laden ritual. Human structural distinctions and status become meaningless within the act of sharing the one bread and one cup and celebrating unique *koinonia*—Christian communitas—among the baptized.[9] If the sacred time and space of worship is the destination of pilgrimage, the Lord's Table is the greatest symbol of sacred transition standing in the center of the community. History and timelessness merge.

> In the Eucharist the Christian assembly truly proclaims its identity as a pilgrim people, a people in transition from the promise to fulfillment. In it the earthly assembly sits at the messianic banquet, relives its origins and partakes of its future. It is the ritual stage on which we act out the eschatological drama of the journey we are undertaking. The Eucharist proclaims that earthly existence itself is a *rite of passage*. In its sacred communitas it witnesses to the transformation which the entire world is called to pass through before history is complete and humanity is reincorporated in the final consummation of the *parousia*.[10]

# Chapter 13
# Caring through the Passage

The counseling pastor sojourns with those passing through the valleys of tumultuous crisis, dramatic developmental shifts, and sometimes baffling and holy intra-psychic states of being. These times of passage may emerge as the result of precipitating events, at the call of an inner, wholly undefined prompting of the spirit, or as part of predictable life changes and transitions. However they come, the pastor is present at the trembling intersections when all seems at stake, which perhaps it is.

David Epston and Michael White suggest a dynamic rather than static view of counseling based on rites of passage concepts. Rather than merely attempting to return a person to a past state of equilibrium, their approach is oriented toward the future. Transformation is expected as a result of the liminal plunge. Liminal categories construe crisis in terms of progress rather than regression.[1] When a static anthropology is assumed, illness represents either breakdown or regression. The implication is that goals become those which attempt to "retrieve and reconstruct the person, thereby returning him or her to a 'good enough' level of functioning."[2] With a dynamic interpretation of the process, the liminal state of being is understood to relate directly to a transition from one status to another (See Appendix 2).

Therapeutic orientations carry their own assumptions and raise their own unique questions in such moments. The Rites of Passage model raises questions which identify the reality from which one has separated, the content which has been revealed during the liminal state of disorganization, and most importantly, an imaginative view of a new future. "This rite of passage analogy can construct the crisis within terms of progress rather than regression without denying its distressing aspects."[3]

The rite of passage metaphor is a useful model in the orientation of therapists and those transitioning from "problematic statuses to unproblematic statuses."[4] It is in liminal space that new possibilities may be explored and persons may access alternative and 'special knowledges' which they have discovered or rediscovered during therapy. The ecstatic experience and participation of the ritual leader or therapist is also indicative of the flow of the process.[5] The degree to which they lose track of time and experience a solidarity, oneness, or identification with the liminal person seeking help is an indication of their informed participation in the liminal process.[6]

The conclusion of the therapeutic process also takes on a different meaning within a rites of passage framework. With reincorporation as the final movement of therapy, the liminal person rejoins others in a familiar social world. It is best marked by rituals of re-entry which include others in an act of celebration and acknowledgment. It is best *not* approached with a "termination as loss" metaphor which only reinforces a sometimes overly privatized "therapeutic micro-world" and individualized concept of personhood. Such therapeutic cultural assumptions are overly isolated, unconnected to primary communities and social systems, and, in Turner's language, "liminoid."[7] A rite of reincorporation may include a narrative review of the therapeutic pilgrimage. This is guided by questions encouraging the sharing of special knowledges discovered in the liminal space of therapy. It may also explore how they arrived at these knowledges.[8] At the time of re-entry, the person in transition may be invited to identify several trusted persons to not only celebrate the conclusion of some particular phase of passage, but to serve as members of an inner circle in the world of ordinary time and space.

A dynamic view of rites of passage is also extremely helpful in crisis counseling. When individuals or systems find themselves within either of the two types of crisis, developmental or situational, it is not only an extremely vulnerable time, but also a very receptive time.[9] "Crisis intervention is not just Band-Aid therapy—it is growth-oriented."[10] This all requires an inward transformation, for "a crisis is what happens within people, what takes place within families as a *response* to that event."[11] As a time of heightened psychological accessibility, "People in crisis are less defensive, more vulnerable, and more open to change than at other times in their lives. . . ."[12]

Even if the severity of problems become such that residential treatment is required, a dynamic model of passage may be adopted. Families and therapists may move beyond the deficit and repair model which is reinforced by the ritual of making a technical diagnosis. This only contributes to removing the problem from the hands of the liminal person. Instead, such a process may be reconceptualized as a "transition between different statuses . . . rites of passage which are ritual processes that involve a transition between life stages or statuses."[13] The three stages of passage—separation, liminality, and reaggregation—may provide the framework for both assessment and treatment. Separation is not only from the family or geography, but from the problem as it is known and experienced in non-liminal time and context. Liminal reality is expected and interpreted as a time of ups and downs, experimentation with trial and error, and confrontation of anomalies which are not consonant with old ways of being, thinking, and acting. Reincorporation comes as the transition ushers an entire family system into a new and hopeful way of being in the world.[14]

In the family therapy setting, a rites of passage model may function as a ritual context through which families pass and from which they emerge in a new state. If the therapist assumes the concepts of this model, the therapy setting often assumes the perimeters as a rite of passage.[15]

In the separation phase, the unique boundaries of a therapeutic setting are established, boundaries which are qualitatively different from the ordinary settings of the family's life. New time and space are provided by a designated, set-apart location, and a set-aside time. Such an alternate time and space often induces a kind of disorientation and confusion of roles as it stands apart from their ordinary reality. This can be very powerful, for it allows for new ways of perceiving as they escape habitual ways of being. The result is often the egalitarian leveling of status. The therapist, as tribal elder, enters the new time and space of confused identities with a special guiding role. As liminal guide, the therapist suggests new alternatives and courses of action which become viable in the betwixt-and-between status of confusion and uncertainty.

As the liminal state within the rites of passage is the most power-laden time for transformation, it is most similar to what some have described as a "flow" state[16]—one of departure from structure and homeostasis, wherein expectations may be challenged, unspeakable subjects discussed, and new roles tested. This may include an experimental playfulness and freedom with roles, thoughts, and behavior which are uncharacteristic of those found in ongoing structural relationships. The highlighting of exceptions and practice of speculation disrupts well-worn and familiar patterns.

When families return to ordinary life, they pass through a stage of reaggregation. If change has been significant, if true passage has taken place, they will re-enter the world of structure, but as new persons together. The presence of a participatory network of life relationships is essential to sustaining and integrating the long-term changes which have taken place.

With the predominant ageism of our culture, we often neglect the shepherding of those who are at the most critical spiritual phases and moments of their lives—the aging. For those of extreme age who have both retained mental acuity and received and cultivated the gift of faith throughout the years, their later years may be ones of tremendous spiritual depth and capacity. As ones commonly placed in the social margin, they are positioned to serve as wise ones for the liminal passages of their younger travelers.

In this margin of age, they face peculiar challenges: illness, loss of freedom and physical capacity, isolation, the vanishing of entire generations of friends, and the ultimate passage—death. Who will dare enter this liminal place with them? The courageous and compassionate liminal guide must enter this land toward which we all move and offer not only listening and company, but "the Christian mystical tradition of spiritual discernment," helping elders to "find the voice to express their religious experience."[17]

A developmental understanding of the life-cycle incorporates the rites of passage in cycles of passages. Development and movement requires separations lest one becomes fixated at one stage or another. After a time of readjustment and transition, the new state of regained structure becomes the platform from which one must make the next shift. It is a movement from pre-liminal through liminal to post-liminal, except that the arrival place—the post-liminal—will necessarily become pre-liminal in another phase. To arrive is to make preparations to depart. There are, in effect, cycles of passages (see Appendix 3). In developmental terms we are literally *ho paragon*.

In spiritual direction the counseling pastor emphasizes the leaning of life toward God: goals, telos, future becoming, and transformation as new creatures. The past is explored to complete the holistic view of the life narrative, to understand the journey to the present and identify reoccurring patterns; but an integrative approach moves beyond mere repair to an eschatological future and hope. It does not yet appear what we shall become, but trust is required to leave the old behind, enter the new uncertain ground on which we have never walked before, and look toward the future. The saga of crucifixion and resurrection, of dying and rising, is bound up in separation, passage, and entry into places on the other side of what we can imagine.

How shall we become ministers of reconciliation for those who are chronically ill, frozen in time, rendered permanently liminal by baffling alternative functions of the mind or body from which they cannot pass? We must dare to enter their state of permanent, involuntary liminality on its own terms. Though we never totally lose hope for some reaggregation into the world of structure, we accept the possibility that some persons may remain in that state. For them our gift must be a special one. It must be a willingness to find redemption *within* their permanent liminality. It must be in the service of participatory ritual presence and spiritual leadership which unearths meaning in a condition from which they may never move. Instead of waiting for redemption in the form of a change which may never come, we look for it in its transcendent form. Rather than expecting a shift from liminality, we look for the unique gifts of insight and depth, however peculiar or irrational in form, which emerge out of the deep pool of their mythic symbol system. Their present remains a place where latent meaning, faith, revelation, and transcendence exist for the chronically separated. As for redemption in historical time and space, the degree of our acceptance of their permanent liminality will be directly related to the vitality of our own eschatology and sense of transcendence.

# Chapter 14
# The Transforming Tribe

One of the direct byproducts of radical empiricism and far-reaching secularization is the stripping of religious and cultural rituals. Modernity has sanitized itself from what it felt to be embarrassing and antiquated leftovers from a superstitious and magic-laden past. The first rituals to be expunged were those which held an explicit supernatural referent. But soon to follow were other social rites which either legitimated the structure of life or even provided for movement within it. Even with such attempts to eliminate ritual, life remains highly ritualized. The only difference now is that the remnants of ritual are practiced without self-conscious understanding. One need only observe the dramatic ritualized behavior surrounding sporting events, the arts, and political campaigns to realize its lingering influence. This is to say nothing of individual ritual life lived out in more or less compulsive terms. Highly self-regulated daily ritual often provides form in the absence of over-arching structures of meaning. And in the absence of rituals we often create them.

In addition, urbanization and suburbanization have created geographically aggregated groups of alienated, disconnected, and suspicious individuals. Lost is a sense of bonded community with mutual accountabilities and benefits. Those who are weak or in need of passage are left to themselves, or sometimes worse, to paid professional surrogates for the support network formally found in friendships, extended families, and religious communities. Troubled persons lack a social world to which they may relate and from which they might decide, act, and be.

The ritually unclean surround us and remain partitioned: the homeless, those of different sexual orientation, persons with addictions of every kind, those with criminal records, and the deinstitutionalized mentally ill. Alienated culture lacks its own transforming center and therefore cannot stand the fearful threat such contemporary lepers represent.

This dominant world view and cultural estrangement has given birth to massive denial. The banishing of ritual and the loss of communitas has contributed to the collective denial of mortality, finitude, and especially suffering. For instance, in a ritual-stripped culture, people who grieve want to do so in utilitarian ways, getting through it quickly without the burden of passing through it. They do not want to be grieving people, but instead people who are over grief. In contrast, ritual enactment requires an uncomfortable entrance into the complete drama of loss. It also provides for deliverance if one is willing to pass through it. The frequently sanitized mechanisms for burying the dead are the most remarkable examples of denial and utilitarian passage in our culture. By means of an artificial and professional environment of disposal, the dead are delivered from sight, but the living remain undelivered.

Sophisticated moderns are sometimes surprised to discover their own thinly veiled envy of less enlightened friends who have religiously and culturally prescribed rites of passage. They longingly watch the adherents of other religious groups grieve and mourn collectively. As one woman said in comparing her rather empty way of dealing with grief to that of a Muslim friend's grieving rituals, "They know what to do." Part of the blindness of pervasive individualism is just this: we dare not allow a center beyond self to suggest anything we have not created ourselves.

In a time of the banishment of ritual, the need for it increases in direct correlation to its absence. Cultic activity and highly formalized sub-groups within the culture proliferate. Vulnerable persons find communitas and leadership for initiation at the edges, though often in coercive and authoritarian form. The result is often not transformation but enslavement. Wherever a vacuum exists it will invariably be filled, even if by liminoid substitutes.

It is no accident that small groups of various kinds have taken on increasing importance. They emerge and flourish in the absence of communitas, and the needs of participants within them are many times satisfied. On the other hand, the more many people flee to groups, the more the goal of communitas often eludes them, for the space and leadership does not foster liminal reality, but rather a liminoid one. There is no ritual movement, no containment, no leadership by initiated elders. Huge portions of our adult population remain uninitiated exactly at a time when they should be providing leadership to new generations and social institutions.

In the church's accommodation to culture, it has often internalized the culture's assessment and verdict on its tradition, ritual life, and even the form of its internal mythos and practice. In a mad and misdirected rush to live out this external verdict, the church has been guilty of abandoning its own symbolic code and voice. The first loss has been one of form, and form is created and sustained by the core beliefs, values, and identity of the religious community. The second loss derives from the church putting aside its distinctive gifts and role in the midst of culture. This results in a loss of the capacity to transform. It became like the culture which was lost, and therefore abdicated any power it may have possessed to heal it.

Many congregations make use of rites of passage to give ritual shape and transformational power to significant transitions of many kinds. They have either never abandoned them or have rediscovered and reclaimed their power. Their community life is marked by ritual enactment which not only teaches in advance through symbolic rehearsal, but also carries the forming story and core of meaning. They become transforming communities for those within them, and a sign to a surrounding culture awash in its own emptiness.

Especially in terms of Christian initiation, the church needs to be less a static institution and more an organic and transforming vessel which shepherds the process of conversion, dying, and being born again. More than simply instructing, it enables persons to enter into a relationship of transforming trust in God in the midst of others also initiated into that same Mystery.[1] This new kind of Christian community is impossible without transforming rites which create initiated Christians. Without authentic initiation, there is no communitas, but rather a weak "communitoid," a highly individualistic, consumeristic, self-serving gathering clamoring for a temporary subjective experience without depth. The collusion on behalf of the church in fabricating these illusions only keeps persons in the structure from whence they have come. Without initiation there is no transformation, conversion, or reconversions.

Confirmational-type initiations have often lapsed into an informational program whose goal is to impart blocks of designated information. Content itself may be important and necessary, but the process is inadequate if it focuses only on transference of information rather than personal transformation in relationship to the sacred and the community of faith. Content alone will not do. If that were the case, the information could simply be sent electronically.

If this current concept of initiation is wanting, so is the arbitrary designation of participants by age, or worse, their grade in school. Determining entry on the basis of either age or grade precludes a focus on the readiness or openness of the person. If the focus would rather be placed on readiness, the boundaries of the current models would be totally revised, if not disassembled.

Rituals during this time should be out of the ordinary, remarkable, dramatic, and extreme. As much attention should be given to the sense of separation from the structure of life and entry into the new, interim community as to memorization, recitation, and survey of content. Periods of sustained silence, prayer, and reflection on the symbols of the faith need to be provided. Pastors' teaching should provoke ambiguity, paradox, and tease out latent questions. The larger issues of God and life should present themselves in graphic and perplexing relief. The time together must be one characterized by mystery. And pastors should clearly begin the process by communicating an expectation that the initiates will not remain unchanged.

Equally important to the initiation process is participation by lay mentors who serve as tribal elders. These persons must be initiated themselves and willing to share the initiation process with others. They must be able to share their own subjective experience of God as well as reciting the guiding metaphors, narratives, and truth of the community. As designated shepherds, they accompany the initiate through the passage, serving as support through the movement to new being.

A direct parallel to present confirmational inadequacies is the dominant model of Christian education which is present in most mainline Protestant churches. As Christian education in the liberal tradition reacted against revivalism and its excesses in the early part of the 20th century, it simultaneously lost important dimensions as it embraced others. It replaced impulses toward conversion and the training of church members to engage in evangelism with a focus on "nurture." It is the concept of nurture which would become the dominant theological and curricular paradigm for decades to come. There were, of course, direct ramifications. As the church became socially disestablished in the culture, it was convinced that maturation itself would provide all that was necessary, as long as it was accompanied by instruction in the public school classroom model. As both conversion and re-conversion were suspect, a chasm between education and evangelism emerged. The expectation that people would be changed in response to the grace of the Gospel diminished. Beneath this model of gradual maturation, of "never having known oneself as anything but Christian," there slept a tacit message: conversion and transformation are unnecessary. Christian education, initiation, and even worship are understood to be occasions for imparting more information and knowing more and more things about God and what it means to grow into a good person. It is but another step in the educational process. And the church received what it came to expect—untransformed Christians and untransformed communities.

In a post-Christendom era, communities of faith and their leaders must recapture commitments to ministries of formation and transformation, allowing for development as well as dramatic and life-changing shifts into and out of liminal time and space. The ability and willingness to expect this, provide for this, will be the measure of the vitality of religious communities in the coming century. Information may be found many places, but nothing short of a dynamic, transformative model of faith will begin to touch people in the many places in which they find themselves throughout their individual and collective journeys.

Congregations which practice rites of passage recognize that grieving rituals mediate loss and usher persons into a new status within the congregation. Death rituals represent the foundations upon which lives stand and begin a process of healing which recognize that no grieving person will remain unchanged. Special rituals on significant anniversaries, such as at the first anniversary of a death, place the grieving person in the courses of memory and time, bringing the reality of both to bear. In time and space, the abstract becomes concrete, and loss is again dramatized and recognized.

In the same way, the church's ministry may offer prescribed or created observances and rituals for other significant passages such as divorce, moving, and retirement. As some life passages are either more socially stigmatized or simply more feared and misunderstood, they call for new attention by faith communities and religious leadership. Wherever there is loss and transition into a liminal state of being, the church should be present through its leaders and members to usher persons into the next chapters of evolving biographies. This healing and hopeful presence may affirm the transformational dimensions of these passages as they accompany persons through them.

# Chapter 15
# The Liminal Domain of War

As the histories of most civilizations have evidenced, the social aspects of harmony and conflict have always existed in a variable tension, manifesting differently according to each culture. This tension has given way to periodic outbreaks of open conflict within a society or between societies. Mythologies, philosophies and theologies have governed decisions to cross the threshold into war as well as guide toward its resolution.[1]

The state of being "at war" is an archetypal experience of social liminality. For the warrior class within each of these societies, war is a rite of passage and warriors, especially in preindustrial traditional societies, were carefully prepared and initiated into their identity as a valued part of the tribe. As they separated from the structure of pre-war into the anti-structure of war, they became liminal persons. As such their identities became charmed and even dangerous. The warrior class took on the impurity of the act of bloodletting on behalf of those for whom they waged war. Symbolic ritual and ceremony mediated the safe transition through this temporary and voluntary form of liminality for both society and its warriors.

Of special importance is the way that ancient, indigenous, non-industrial societies provided for reincorporation of the warrior into post-liminal life after war. Elaborate and often lengthy rituals and ceremonies marked both the departure and the return of warriors. Those traditional practices existed not only to assist warriors in their dramatic transition back into the structure of their tribe, but to protect the tribe from the contagion and danger accumulated in the act of war-making. The warriors were never left to transition by themselves.[2]

Without rituals of return, elder leadership by the initiated, and time to adjust to a new state of being, warriors are much less likely to return to civilian life as whole persons. They are prohibited from experiencing the transformation that may be possible through rites of passage rituals. Without those communal mechanisms of return they become stuck in an involuntary state of permanent liminality, a war that never ends, and a war they can never leave.

In addition, for the warrior who has experienced a rare and intense form of communitas during war, exit from that community of the liminal often results in a profound sense of isolation. They have become disconnected from those with whom they shared an assumed world. In fact, as the liminal terrain of war comes to assume its own normality, separation from war into civilian life represents a new and different form of liminalty.

No person is unaffected by their experience of war; it changes them forever. What is often said by the families of those who went and returned is very true: "My loved one left one person and came back another."

A permanent alteration of the heart and soul takes place whenever life is taken, whether individually or collectively. In the case of atrocities and the blind rage that often transpires in the fog of war, the soul wounding is compounded. Whenever the warrior violates an inner moral code, a sense of guilt and shame pervades. This is often accompanied by a sense of having been betrayed by those who sent them. It seems as though the inner person, the soul, has been lost forever, irredeemable.[3]

As the warrior emerges from those liminal places and a resulting wounding of the soul, the only path to forgiveness, restoration, and reconciliation is a spiritual and communal one. The model for this healing process may resemble a counterpart to ancient practices, the rites of passage model, a present day ritual process based on the concepts of liminality.

If contemporary society and faith communities are to create intentional pathways of welcome, support and healing, they will need to fashion safe set-apart time and space for transformation that includes initiated mentoring, symbolic ceremonies and rituals that allow for purification, opportunities for story-telling, preparation of the family and tribe to receive them, and pilgrimages of reconciliation.

A prerequisite to establishing such pathways is changing public perception of the warrior's journey. That new understanding includes an awareness of where that journey has led and the kind of wounding that has taken place as a result. A new awareness in society may contribute to a renewed resolve and commitment to participate in the healing.

Sources of healing also include the arts in their many forms. Artistic creation often reveals and expresses the deepest recesses of emotion. One of the most remarkable examples in our time is that of *The War Requiem* by Benjamin Britten. Completed in 1962, the work was commissioned for the rededication of Coventry Cathedral. Britten's expansive creation parallels the two cathedral structures that sit adjacent to one another; the bombed out ruin of the original cathedral and its newly constructed successor. As a parallel to those dual architectural edifices, he constructed a spacious musical composition that held its own powerful duality.

In contrast with earlier, more heroic war presentations of national resolve and vigor, Britten wed the conventional aspects of the Requiem Mass with the somber poetry of Wilfred Owen, a writer who fought in the trenches of the First World War. Though his poetry would survive the war, Owen would not; he was killed shortly before the Armistice was signed.[4]

Britten's *Requiem* alternates the realism of Owen's agonizing verse with a haunting proclamation of faith set in the traditional movements of the Mass. By allowing the voices to collide, his work assists the listener in simultaneously experiencing both the horror of war and a transcendent hope of its redemption. Owen's voice is muddy, a prophetic statement from the trenches of cynicism and despair. The historic strains of the Requiem Mass, on the other hand, restate truths that may transcend any tragedy.

Britten's great liminal collision takes place from the very beginning, in the first movement, the *Requiem Aeternam*:

*From the Mass, the Chorus:*

Requiem aeternam dona eis, Domine;
et lux perpetua luceat eis.

(Lord, grant them eternal rest;
and let the perpetual light shine upon them.)

*And then the Boys Choir:*

Te decet hymnus, Deus in Sion:
et tibi reddetur votum in Jerusalem;
exaudi orationem meam,
ad te omnis caro veniet.

(Thou shalt have praise in Zion, of God: and homage shall bepaid to thee in Jerusalem; hear my prayer,
all flesh shall come before Thee.)

*From Wilfred Owen, solo Tenor:*

What passing bells for these who die as cattle?
Only the monstrous anger of the guns.
Only the stuttering rifles' rapid rattle can patter out their hasty orisons.
No mockeries for them from prayers or bells,
Nor any voice of mourning save the choirs,
The shrill, demented choirs of wailing shells;
And bugles calling for them from sad shires.
What candles may be held to speed them at all?
Not in the hands of boys, but in their eyes
Shall shine the holy glimmers of good-byes.
The pallor of girls' brows shall be their pall;
Their flowers the tenderness of silent minds,
And each slow dusk a drawing-down of blinds.[5]

Somewhere between two contrasting cathedrals, one ruined and ancient and the other modern, and at the intersection of two voices, one realistically despondent and the other hopeful, an interval of time and space exists in which healing and hope become possible. This is the healing power of art expressing the liminal in the domain of the liminal.

The interaction between two forms of liminality makes the difference: sacred traditional texts rise up from the liminal edges in their own transcendent ways, and verse such as that from Owen reflects the liminal location of war. Both liminal texts, liminal for different reasons, speak to and with one another.

What is required for the healing path of the returning warrior? There must always be ample provision for truth telling just as Owen told the truth. Concrete and particular truth telling are nested among the larger, mythical, archetypal stories, such as are found in the Mass. This places historical phenomena within a larger, universal matrix. It is then that ritual leadership crafts and conducts passage through the healing domain, never leaving that responsibility to the one who at that moment of reentry needs to receive more than lead.

The healing path of the warrior may be walked most powerfully with those sharing communitas, brothers and sisters who have passed through the same liminal domain of war. Only they can truly know what war requires, how it changes a person forever, and the ways that truly make for peace. Today we face an additional complexity related to war and liminality. If the nature of war is best understood through a liminal lens, present day changes in the way war is executed – its formlessness, absence of defined battlefields and fronts, and the blurring of combatants and civilians – all contribute to its emergence as a form of permanent liminality, something that takes place in a "perpetual potential war zone."[6] What sense can a society or group of societies make of such a perpetual reality? How can a warrior pass through something that has no beginning or end? Do citizens and warriors alike simply adopt permanent liminality is the new normal, the antistructure that has become our structure? If we are able to see it for what it is, can a new transformation emerge, one equal to the dilemma?

# *Epilogue*
# The Minister as Liminal Being

Pastors of local congregations today face a daunting and seemingly impossible array of tasks and roles. They have received from their own theologies and traditions through the centuries, as well as from the culture surrounding them, a layered set of complex expectations. This stratigraphy of ministerial roles, including saint, priest, healer, preacher, builder of empires, missionary, manager, counselor, charismatic leader, and teacher, is an inheritance often more confusing than clarifying. Such a conglomeration of roles is impossible to fulfill, even if one aspired to do so, and has contributed to what has become a crisis in ministerial identity.[1] However confusing the array of roles, and however one comes to select those which seem most central to the pastoral office, the role of liminal ritual leader and guide has broad and direct application. There is no pastoral role which does not deal directly with endings, transitions, and transformed beginnings.

The vocation of religious leader, known by interior and logic-defying call, set apart by and for and from the community of faith, is itself a state of permanent liminality. Even as a part of an established community, life is itinerant. This pastoral liminality exists between worlds: the religious leader is a part of, yet distinct from, the community served, symbolizing and mediating powers unknown, a sign of the unity among the initiated and their communitas, a reminder of the transience of all things. A sense of transcendence derives from otherness even as immanence emerges from the incarnate love of souls.

Truth, insight, and wisdom spring from scripture, tradition, reason, and experience, to be sure, but not only from these. Such realities are also pneumatic in nature and origin; the spirit provides creative vitality and transformative power beyond all rational, absolute, or static categories.

As a liminal being, the religious leader intimately knows liminal reality as one already initiated. As such, he or she may serve as ritual leader in the center of the liminal states of individuals or groups. Whether standing beside the open casket, around the campfire at a summer camp for youth, in the home of the mentally ill, in the pulpit speaking a word to the many in the midst of collective confusion, in the classroom teaching searching students, or among those entering the second half of life, the ritual leader facilitates passage and transformation. It may be with those who choose to do so, or with those who have no option; but however we arrive at the threshold, the only way to journey is through the wilderness and across the river, passing from death into new life.

# *Appendix 1*
# Biblical References in which the Number Forty Serves as Symbol of Liminal Reality

The number 40 (forty) holds symbolic connotation of transitional and interim periods of time. The designated periods are not only situated between events, but serve a transformational function. Sacred time is marked by beginning and ending points within which the individual or community is to pass through and be recreated by significant change.

**Genesis 7:4-8:6**

The flood which lasts for forty days and forty nights serves as interim state between an old, corrupted world, and the birth of a new, cleansed one.

**Genesis 50:3**

The death ritual surrounding the demise of Jacob requires forty days of transitional embalming.

**Exodus 16:35; Num. 14:33, 34; 32:13; Deut. 2:7; 8:2; 29:5; Josh. 5:6; Neh. 9:21; Ps. 95:10; Amos 2:10; 5:25; Acts 7:36, 42; 13:18; Hebrews 3:10**

The Israelites wander in the wilderness for forty years in passage from the oppression of Egypt to the land-giving of Canaan.

**Exodus 24:18; 34:28; Deut. 9:9; 9:11; 9:18; 9:25; 10:10**

Moses is suspended on the holy mountain for forty days and forty nights, symbolically situated between heaven and earth. During this time he fasts and receives sacred knowledge which he records as the decalogue.

**Numbers 13:25**

The exploration of the multi-faceted dimensions of Canaan takes forty days, and must take place before the Israelites may cross over.

**Judges 3:11; 5:31; 8:20**

Occasions of interim peace between conflicts last forty years.

**Judges 13:1**

The Israelites are controlled by the Philistines for forty years as a punishment.

**I Samuel 17:16**

For forty days, Goliath taunts the Israelites.

**I Kings 19:8**

In flight for his life, Elijah travels forty days and forty nights toward the holy mountain of Horeb. On the way he is strengthened by a visionary dream and the ministrations of an angelic figure within it.

**Ezekiel 4:6**

As a part of one of his ecstatic visions, the prophet is instructed to lie on his right side for forty days, each day representing one year of Judah's rebellion. The symbolic act vicariously takes the sins of the people upon himself.

**Ezekiel 29:11-13**

The prophesies against Egypt include a desolation of forty years.

**Jonah 3:4**

The time between warning and catastrophe in Nineveh is forty days.

**Matthew 4:2, Mark 1:13, Luke 4:2**

Jesus' fasting and temptation in the wilderness lasts forty days and nights.

**Acts 1:3**

Resurrection appearances occur in a forty day interval between resurrection and ascension.

## Forty Year Reigns

| | |
|---|---|
| I Samuel 4:18 | Eli as judge |
| II Samuel 5:4 | David as king |
| I Kings 11:42 | Solomon as king |
| II Kings 12:1 | Jehoash as king |
| II Chronicles 24:1 | Joash as king |

# *Appendix 2*
# The Rites of Passage Model

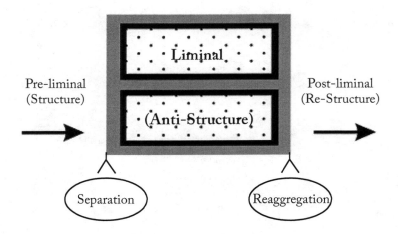

# *Appendix 3*
# The Cyclical Rites of
# Passage Model

A s the Rites of Passage model is a dynamic one, the arrival point of post-liminal reality always becomes the platform from which one will later launch into yet another cycle of renewal and transformation. This provides a conceptual framework that is compatible with both developmental and conversional frameworks.

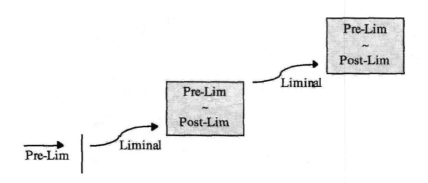

# *Appendix 4*
# Scriptural Resources

The foundational narratives from the scriptures shed light not only on the human condition but on the transcendent realities of God. In the service of preaching, teaching, and guiding in liminal times, the pastor offers and interprets them to the individual and community in relation to the reality through which they pass. Following are texts which directly reflect liminal reality in its many dimensions.

| | |
|---|---|
| Genesis 3 | Eden and Beyond |
| Genesis 6-8 | The Death and Rebirth of the World |
| Exodus 13:17-22 | Crossing Over |
| Exodus 19 | Holy Mountains |
| Exodus 32 | Flight From Wilderness |
| Ruth 1 | Bonded Beyond Blood |
| I Samuel 3 | Elders, the Initiated, and Ritual Leadership |
| Job 1 and 42 | The Caldron of Transformation |
| Isaiah 6:1-8 | Ecstasy and Agony |
| Isaiah 40 | Of Return and Renewal |
| Matthew 4 | Desert Decisions |
| Luke 9:28-36 | Knowing Beyond Sense |
| Acts 2:1-5 | Together In One Place |
| Romans 6:3-11 | The Drama of Death and Life |
| I Corinthians 13:8-12 | Face to Face |
| II Corinthians 12:1-6 | Beyond Time, Beyond Space |
| Revelation 21 | The Alpha and Omega |

# Notes

## Preface

1. Agnes Horvath, Bjorn Thomassen, and Harald Wydra, *Breaking Boundaries: Varieties of Liminality* (New York & Oxford: Berghahn Books, 2015).

## Chapter 1. Anthropology and the Rites of Passage

2. Arnold van Gennep, *The Rites of Passage* (London: Routledge and Kegan Paul, 1960).
3. Ibid., 18.
4. Ibid., 189.
5. See Juha Pentikainen, "The Symbolism of Liminality," in *Religious Symbols and Their Functions,* based on papers read at the Symposium on Religious Symbols and their Functions held at Abo 28-30 August, 1978 (Uppsala: Almqvist & Wiksell International, 1979), 154-167. He makes distinctions between the three main categories of rites: rites of passage, calendar rites and rites of crisis. Rites of passage are individual, nonrepeatable and predictable; calendar rites are collective, repeatable, and predictable; and crisis rites are individual or collective, nonrepeatable and nonpredictable.
6. van Gennep, 21.
7. Ibid., 191.
8. Ibid.
9. Robert N. Bellah, "Religious Pluralism and Religious Truth," the 1994-95 Bainton Lecture at Yale Divinity School, in *Reflections,* Vol. 90, No. 2 (New Haven: Yale Divinity School, Summer-Fall 1995), 9.
10. Ibid., 10.
11. van Gennep, 189-90.
12. Victor Turner, "Betwixt and Between: The Liminal Period in Rites of Passage," in *The Forest of Symbols* (Ithaca: Cornell University Press, 1967), 93-111.
13. Ibid., 93.
14. Ibid.
15. Ibid.
16. Ibid., 94.
17. Ibid.
18. Ibid., 95.
19. Ibid., 97.

20. Ibid.
21. Mary Douglas, *Purity and Danger* (New York: Frederick A. Praeger, 1966).
22. Ibid., 95.
23. Ibid., 96.
24. Ibid., 96-97.
25. Claude Levi-Strauss, *The Savage Mind* (Chicago: University of Chicago Press, 1966).
26. Victor Turner, *The Ritual Process: Structure and Anti-Structure* (New York: Aldine Publishing Company, 1969).
27. Ibid., 97.
28. Ibid., 102-104.
29. Ibid., 96.
30. Catherine Bell, *Ritual Theory, Ritual Practice* (New York: Oxford University Press, 1992).
31. Ibid., 31.
32. Ibid., 171.

## Chapter 2. Life, Death and Rebirth

1. Emile Durkheim, *The Elementary Forms of the Religious Life* (New York: The Free Press, 1915)
2. Ibid., 54.
3. Ibid.
4. Dario Zadra, "Victor Turner's Theory of Religion: Toward an Analysis of Symbolic Time," in *Anthropology and the Study of Religion* (Chicago: Center for the Scientific Study of Religion, 1984), 96.
5. Mircea Eliade, *Rites and Symbols of Initiation* (New York: Harper & Row, 1958).
6. Ibid., 62.
7. Ibid., 195.
8. Beldon Lane, *Landscapes of the Sacred* (Paulist Press, 1988), 152-160.
9. Mircea Eliade, *The Sacred and the Profane* (New York: Harcourt Brace Jovanovich, 1959), 191.
10. Ibid.
11. Mircea Eliade, *Myth and Reality* (New York: Harper & Row, 1963), 79.
12. Ibid., 80.
13. Ibid., 81.
14. Mircea Eliade, *Shamanism: Archaic Techniques of Ecstasy* (New York: Pantheon Books, 1964), 33.
15. R.L. Stirrat, "Sacred Models," in *Man*, Vol. 19, No. 2 (London: Royal Anthropological Institute of Great Britain and Ireland, 1984), 199-200. The problem of the projection of the social onto the religious plane model is found in exceptions; too much of what is contained in the religious sphere does not fit neatly into the social construction of reality, including its values.
16. See Claude Welch, *Protestant Thought in the Nineteenth Century, Vol. I* (New Haven: Yale University Press, 1972), 172. In a movement away from Hegalian idealism, the human is exalted as center. Thought does not precede sensory reality, rather the divine is the human and the human is divine, but the human is the starting place. For Feuerbach, the human self objectifies itself, projecting itself onto the infinite. Sacred time and space in his sense is an overcoming of alienation by removing the supernatural, and recognizing the self as center of space and time.
17. Stirrat, 202.

18. Ibid., 204.
19. Ibid., 209.
20. For the hermeneutical adaptation of the concept of liminality in literary criticism, see Rees Conrad Douglas, "Liminality and Conversion in Joseph and Aseneth," in *Journal for the Study of the Pseudepigrapha*, No. 3 (Oct. 1988), 31-42, and Mark McVann, "The Passion in Mark: Transformation Ritual," in *Biblical Theology Bulletin*, 18 (J/1988), 96-101; for an application of liminality in the explanation of historical context related to narrative plot, see Leo Perdue, "Liminality as a Social Setting for Wisdom Instructions," in *Zeitschrift fur die Alttestamentliche Wissenschaft*, 93, No. 1 (1981), 114-126; for an interesting application to Christology and culture, see Mark Taylor, "In Praise of Shaky Ground: The Liminal Christ and Cultural Pluralism," in *Theology Today*, 43, No. 1 (Apr. 1986), 36-51.

# Chapter 3. On Being There all the Time

1. Victor Turner, *The Ritual Process*, 107.
2. Ibid., 111-112.
3. See Warren Carter, "Households and Discipleship: A Study of Matthew 19-20," in *Journal for the Study of the New Testament*, Supplement Series 103 (Sheffield: Sheffield Academic Presss, 1994), 49-55, for a discussion of the function of permanent liminality in Matthew's Gospel. Matthew reflects a subtle interaction between those who are involuntarily marginal due to position in the social strata of the Roman empire and the voluntarily marginal who are called to a separated and itinerant life. The temporal framework of Matthaean discipleship begins with dramatic separation from structure in the dramatic call stories and transitions to the concluding aggregations of the expected parousia. Disciples live in between these two boundaries of call and parousia, separation and aggregation, in a liminal anti-structure existence. Matthew 19-20 guides the reader to an identity grounded in liminal communitas which includes a radical egalitarianism. This egalitarian way of life overturns the hierarchial household code fundamental to first-century life.
4. Phillas Maack, "Feminine Behavior, Radical Action," in *Signs: Journal of Women in Culture and Society*, No. 3 (Spr. 1986), 457-477.
5. Gerd Theissen, *Sociology of Early Palestinian Christianity* (Philadelphia: Fortress Press, 1978). Theissen originated the discussion of itinerancy and the Jesus movement, as well as making the connection to Cynicism for the first time.
6. John Dominic Crossan, *The Historical Jesus: The Life of a Mediterranean Peasant* (San Francisco: Harper Collins, 1991), 74-76.
7. Ibid., 79.
8. Ibid., 81.
9. Ibid.
10. Ibid., 421.
11. Ibid. This difference ultimately leads Crossan to draw a crucial distinction between the Cynics and Jesus movement. Whereas the Cynics aimed toward self-sufficiency, the followers of Jesus practiced a radical dependency. In liminal categories it might be said that the Cynics sought a liminality without communitas while the Jesus people embraced both.
12. Ibid., 422.

13. Theissen, 8.
14. Ibid.
15. Ibid., 15.
16. Stephen J. Patterson, *The Gospel of Thomas and Jesus* (Sonoma, CA: Polebridge Press, 1993), 159.
17. Ibid.
18. Ibid., 160.
19. Ibid., 161.
20. Ibid., 166.
21. Ibid., 163.
22. For an early classic study on Gnosticism, see Hans Jonas, *The Gnostic Religion* (Boston: Beacon Press, 1958), esp. 48-99, the description of the "alien" god and its relationship to the transient sojourn of the homesick stranger in this world.
23. Ingvild Gilhus, "Gnosticism—A Study in Liminal Symbolism," in *Numen* (31 July 1984), 106-128.
24. Ibid., 109.
25. Ibid., 110.
26. For exploration of dominant Gnostic theologies and anthropologies which led to ascetic practice and relationship to the world, see Giulia Sfameni Gasparro, "Asceticism and Anthropology: *Enkrateia* and 'Double Creation' in Early Christianity," 130; and for an extended discussion of the social function of asceticism in relation to anti-structure, Richard Valantasis, "A Theory of the Social Function of Asceticism," 544-551; both are found in Vincent L. Wimbush and Richard Valantasis, ed., *Asceticism* (New York: Oxford University Press, 1995). Valentasis develops a theory of asceticism within which the social position of anti-structure serves to transform the individual in relation to culture as well as re-envision a new world.
27. Gilhus, 119.
28. Ibid., 120.
29. Ibid., 122-23.
30. Pinchas Giller, *The Enlightened Will Shine: Symbolization and Theurgy in the Later Strata of the Zohar* (Albany: State University of New York Press, 1993), 22.
31. Arthur Green, *Tormented Master: A Life of Rabbi Nahman of Bratzlar* (Tuscaloosa: University of Alabama Press, 1979), 229.

## Chapter 4. The Inside of the Outside

1. Mircea Eliade, *Shamanism*, 33.
2. William Baird, *1 Corinthians and 2 Corinthians* (Atlanta: John Knox Press, 1980), 104-105.
3. Mircea Eliade, *Myths, Dreams and Mysteries* (New York: Harper & Row, 1960), 78.
4. Emile Durkheim, *The Elementary Forms of the Religious Life*, 258.
5. Ibid., 259.
6. Cervantes, *The Man of La Mancha*.
7. Michel Foucault, *Madness and Civilization* (New York: Vintage Books, 1988).
8. Ibid., 78.
9. Ibid., 115.
10. Ibid., 116.
11. Ibid., 11.

12. William James, *The Varieties of Religious Experience* (New York: The New American Library, 1958).

13. Ibid., 24.

14. Ibid., 24-25.

15. Ibid., 37, 292.

16. Ibid., 292-93.

17. Ibid., 298.

18. Ioan M. Lewis, *Ecstatic Religion* (Baltimore: Penguin Books, 1971), 46.

19. Ibid., 185.

20. Ibid., 188.

21. Ibid., 192.

22. American Psychiatric Association, *Diagnostic and Statistical Manual of Mental Disorders-DSM-5* (Washington, D.C.: American Psychiatric Association, 1994), 304.

23. William Ralph Inge, *Christian Mysticism* (New York: Scribner's, 1899), 335.

24. Kieran Kavanaugh and Otilio Rodriguez, eds., *The Collected Works of St. Teresa of Avila* (Washington D.C.: Institute of Carmelite Studies, 1976), 74.

25. Ibid., 518.

26. Evelyn Underhill, *Mysticism* (New York: Dutton, 1961), 76.

27. Kenneth Stifler, Joanne Greer, William Sneck and Robert Dovenmuehle, "An Empirical Investigation of the Discriminability of Reported Mystical Experiences Among Religious Contemplatives, Psychotic Inpatients, and Normal Adults," in *Journal for the Scientific Study of Religion*, Vol. 32, No. 4 (1993), 366-372. In a study comparing thirty psychotic patients with religious delusions, thirty senior members of various contemplative/mystical groups and a control group comprising thirty persons, the similarities and differences of the groups were studied. In terms of altered states of awareness and perception, there existed little qualitative difference between the mystics and persons experiencing a florid psychotic episode, though both mystics and psychotics scored much higher on the Hood Mysticism Scale than the normal population. The psychotic group scored much higher than either mystics or normals in ego grasping (EGO scale). Both psychotics and mystics scored higher than normals in narcissistic absorption (NPI scores). Results of the research suggest that there is little difference in subjective experience between mystics and psychotics, but a great difference in personality structure. The psychotic experience is one defined by rigid ego structure, excessive control, dualistic separations, and striving. Authentic mystical experience which is free of psychopathology induces integration, fluidity, and openness. This difference may explain the contrast between the mostly voluntary nature of mystical experience and the involuntary nature of psychotic experience. The narcissism scales are elevated for both mystics and psychotics as compared to normals. Though the meaning of this is yet to be fully determined, the powerful subjective states of both groups might naturally lead to greater self-consciousness. In mystical experience free of ego grasping, though, this intense subjective experience usually leads to increased self-negation in relation to the transcendent and compassion toward other creatures.

28. Robert Fishman, "Transmigration, Liminality, and Spiritualist Healing," in *Journal of Religion and Health*, Vol. 19, No. 3 (Fall 1980).

29. Ibid., 218.

30. Ibid., 219-20.

## Chapter 5. In Our Stars or in Our Genes

1. Eugene d'Aquili, Charles Laughlin, Jr., and John McManus, *The Spectrum of Ritual: A Biogenetic Structural Analysis* (New York: Columbia University Press, 1979), 4.
2. Ibid., 29.
3. Ibid., 33.
4. Ibid., 51.
5. Barbara Lex, "The Neurobiology of Ritual Trance," in Eugene d'Aquili, Charles Laughlin, Jr., and John McManus, *The Spectrum of Ritual: A Biogenetic Structural Analysis* (New York: Columbia University Press, 1979), 118.
6. Ibid., 119.
7. Ibid., 120.
8. Ibid., 140.
9. Ibid., 140.
10. Ibid., 141.
11. Victor Turner, "Body, Brain and Culture," in *Zygon,* Vol. 18, No. 3 (September 1983).
12. Ibid., 237.
13. Ibid., 243.
14. Ibid., 243.
15. Eugene d'Aquili and Andrew Newberg, "Liminality, Trance, and Unitary States in Ritual and Meditation," in *Studia Liturgica* 23, No. 1 (1993), 2-34.
16. Ibid., 4.
17. Ibid., 10.
18. Ibid., 34.

## Chapter 6. Continuity and Context

1. Victor Turner, "Liminality, Kabbalah, and the Media," in *Religion* 15 (1985), 205-217.
2. Ibid., 216.
3. Ibid., 216.
4. Elihu Katz and Daniel Dayan, "Media Events: On the Experience of Not Being There," in *Religion* 15 (1985), 305-314.
5. Ibid., 305.
6. Ibid., 305.
7. Ibid., 311-313.
8. Erik Cohen, "Tourism as Play," in *Religion* 15 (1985), 305-314.
9. Geoffrey Chaucer, *The Canterbury Tales,* ed. Donald Howard (New York: Mentor and Plume Books, 1969).
10. Victor Turner, "Death and the Dead in the Pilgrimage Process," in *Religious Encounters With Death* (University Park: Pennsylvania State University Press, 1977), 24-25.
11. Frederick B. Jonassen, "The Inn, the Cathedral, and the Pilgrimage of the Canterbury Tales, 1" in Fein, Faybin, and Braeger, eds., *Rebels and Rivals* (Kalamazoo: Medieval Institute Publications, 1991), 1-5.
12. John Naisbitt, *Global Paradox* (New York: William Morrow and Company, Inc., 1994), 23.
13. Susan Sered, "Rachel's Tomb: Societal Liminality and the Revitalization of a Shrine," in *Religion* 19 (1989), 27-40.
14. Ibid., 27.

## Chapter 7. Present–Day Passage

1. Claude Levi-Strauss, *Structural Anthropology* (New York: Anchor Books, 1967), 200.
2. Ibid., 195.
3. Ibid., 197.
4. Ibid., 198.
5. Ibid., 227.
6. Ibid., 200.
7. Don Browning, *Religious Thought and the Modern Psychologies* (Philadelphia: Fortress Press, 1987), 91.
8. Ibid.
9. Jan and Murray Stein, "Psychotherapy, Initiation and the Mid-life Transition," in Louise Cams Mahdi, ed., *Betwixt and Between* (La Salle, Illinois: Open Court Pub. Co., 1987), 289.
10. Ibid., 295.
11. Walter V. Odajnyk, "The Meaning of Depression at Significant Stages of Life," in Louise Cams Mahdi, ed., *Betwixt and Between* (La Salle, Illinois: Open Court Pub. Co., 1987), 289.
12. Robert Moore, "Contemporary Psychotherapy as Ritual Process: An Initial Reconnaissance," in *Zygon* 18 (S. 1983), 283-294.
13. Ibid., 288.
14. Ibid., 293.
15. Volney Gay, "Ritual and Self-Esteem in Victor Turner and Heinz Kohut," in *Zygon* 18 (S. 1983), 271-282, esp. 274-275.
16. Ibid., 276.
17. Robert L. Moore, "Ritual, Sacred Space, and Healing: The Psychoanalyst as Ritual Elder," in Nathan Schwartz-Salant and Murray Stein, eds., *Liminality and Transitional Phenomena* (Wilmette, Illinois: Chiron Publications, 1991), 23-24.
18. Ibid., 27.
19. Ibid., 29.

## Chapter 8. More than Madness

1. DSM-5, 94-95.
2. Ibid.
3. For further background research in the etiology of these disorders see Glenn Shean, *Schizophrenia: An Introduction to Research and Theory* (New York: University Press of America, 1979). The *Biophysical* model focuses on genetics in familial transmission, and biochemical explanations of brain dysfunction. *Behavioral* theorists limit definitions and treatment to the arena of learned and changed behavior. *Cognitive* theorists deal with irregular thought patterns and attempt to change or alter those patterns. *Sociopsychological* theorists view schizophrenia as a social phenomenon rather than a disease or intra-psychic process. *Family systems* theorists lodge the problem in disturbance in the interactive patterns of the family. *Psychodynamic* theorists identify cause in arrested development at key psychosexual stages. *Interpersonal* theorists find inadequate ways of relating to others as key. *Psychological* approaches relate early childhood experiences of intense anxiety, frustration, absence of warmth and security to the condition. And *Existential Phenomenological* approaches related it to fundamental ontological structures of one's very being.

4. DSM-5, 291.

5. DSM-5, 295.

6. Ibid.

7. Mary Gerhart and Allan Russell, *Metaphoric Process* (Fort Worth: TCU Press, 1994), 4.

8. Thomas S. Kuhn, *The Structure of Scientific Revolutions,* 2nd ed. (Chicago: University of Chicago Press, 1970), ix.

9. Morris Berman, *The Reenchantment of the World* (Ithaca: Cornell University Press, 1981), 17.

10. Julian Silvermann, "Shamans and Acute Schizophrenia," in *American Anthropologist,* Vol. 69, No. 1 (February 1967).

11. Westermeyer, Joseph, ed., *Anthropology and Mental Health* (The Hague: Mouton Publishers, 1976).

12. Otto Billig, B.G. Burton-Bradley, and Ellen Doermann, "Schizophrenic Graphic Expression and Tribal Art in New Guinea," in Joseph Westermeyer, ed., *Anthropology and Mental Health* (The Hague: Mouton Publishers, 1976).

13. Ibid., 246.

14. Silvano Ariete, *The Intrapsychic Self* (New York: Basic Books, 1976), 61-69.

15. Carl Jung, *Psychology and Religion* (New York: Vail-Ballou Press, 1938), 4.

16. Ibid., 63-64.

17. John W. Perry, *Roots of Renewal in Myth and Madness: the Meaning of Psychotic Episodes* (San Francisco: Jossey-Bass Publishers, 1976).

18. Ibid., ix.

19. Ibid., 13.

20. Ibid., 11.

21. Ibid., x.

22. Ibid., 82.

23. Ibid., 13.

24. Ibid., 17.

25. Francis Macnab, *Estrangement and Relationship* (Bloomington, IN: Indiana University Press, 1965).

26. Ibid., 164-65.

27. Ibid., 166.

28. James A. Hall, "The Watcher at the Gates of Dawn: The Transformation of the Self in Liminality and by the Transcendent Function," in Nathan Schwartz-Lalant and Murray Stein, eds., *Liminality and Transitional Phenomena* (Wilmette, Illinois: Chiron Publications, 1991), 41.

29. Ibid., 45.

30. Ibid., 47.

## *Part II Introduction*

1. Paul Pruyser, *The Minister as Diagnostician* (Philadelphia: The Westminster Press, 1976), 60-79.

2. Charles Gerkin, *The Living Human Document* (Nashville: Abingdon Press, 1984), 105.

3. Charles Gerkin, *Widening the Horizons* (Philadelphia: The Westminster Press, 1986), 26.

## Chapter 9. The Liminal Locale of Hospitalization

1. Ann Hallstein, "Spiritual Opportunities in the Liminal Rites of Hospitalization," in *Journal of Religion and Health* 31 (Fall 1992), 247-254, esp. 247.
2. Ibid., 252.
3. Ibid., 253-254.
4. Luis F. Garcia, "The Portrait of a Man: A Case Study of Lance Corporal Tirado's Liminal Transition and the Pastoral Counselor as a Guide Through Liminality," in *Dissertation* (Claremont: School of Theology at Claremont, 1994).

## Chapter 10. Higher Education as Liminal Domain

1. Christopher Moody, "Students, Chaplaincy and Pilgrimage," in *Theology* 89 (Nov. 1986), 440-447.
2. Ibid., 447.

## Chapter 11. In Season and Out of Season

1. I am indebted to Dr. Joseph Jeter, retired professor of homiletics at Brite Divinity School, Fort Worth, Texas, for clarifying issues and tasks which are related to preaching in times of crisis.

## Chapter 12. Liturgy Betwixt and Between

1. J. Randall Nichols, "Worship as Anti-Structure: the Contribution of Victor Turner," in *Theology Today*, Vol. XLI, No. 4, 404.
2. Ibid., 405.
3. Ibid.
4. Ibid., 407.
5. Jean-Pierre Ruiz, "Betwixt and Between on the Lord's Day: Liturgy and the Apocalypse," in *The Society of Biblical Literature 1992 Seminar Papers*, ed. E. Lovering (Atlanta: Scholars Press, 1992), 663.
6. Marchita B. Mauck, "The Liminal Space of Ritual and Art," in John R. May, ed., *The Bent World: Essays on Religion and Culture* (Atlanta: Scholars Press, 1979), 149-157.
7. Don Edgerton, "Worship and Transformation, 1'in *The Chicago Theological Seminary Register* (Chicago: Chicago Theological Seminary, Fall 1985), 14.
8. Ibid., 16.
9. Lawrence Goodwin, "Eucharist and Liminality," in *AFER*, Vol. 21 (Eldoret, Kenya: AMECEA Pastoral Institute, 1979), 350-351.
10. Ibid., 351.

## Chapter 13. Caring through the Passage

1. Michael White and David Epston, *Narrative Means to Therapeutic Ends* (New York: W.W. Norton & Company, 1990), 8.
2. Ibid., 7.
3. Ibid., 8.
4. David Epston and Michael White, "Consulting Your Consultants: The Documentation of Alternative Knowledges," in *Experience, Contradiction, Narrative*

*and Imagination: Selected Papers of David Epston and Michael White, 1989-1991* (South Australia: Dulwich Centre Publications, 1991), 13.

5. Christopher Bollas, *The Shadow of the Object* (New York: Columbia University Press, 1987), 10: "When I practice psychoanalysis, seeing ten people a day five days a week, my daily frame of mind is akin to a meditative state. . . . I often find that although I am working on an idea without knowing exactly what it is that I think, I am engaged in thinking an idea struggling to have me think it."

6. Ibid., 13.

7. Ibid., 14-15.

8. Ibid., 17.

9. Howard Stone, *Crisis Counseling* (Minneapolis: Fortress Press, 1993), 13.

10. Ibid., 14.

11. Ibid., 21.

12. Ibid., 26-27.

13. Michael Durrant, *Residential Treatment* (New York: W.W. Norton & Company, 1993), 12-16.

14. Ibid., 18.

15. R. Rogers Kobak and David B. Waters, "Family Therapy as a Rite of Passage: Play's the Thing," in *Family Process*, Vol. 23, No. 1 (Walwick, NJ: Family Process, Inc., 1984), 89-100.

16. Ibid., 97.

17. Drew Christiansen, "And Your Elders Will Dream Dreams: Aging, Liminality and the Church's Ministry," in Sanks and Coleman, eds., *Reading the Signs of the Times* (New York: Paulist Press, 1995), 131.

## Chapter 14. The Transforming Tribe

1. Aidan Kavanagh, "Christian Initiation," *Made, Not Born: New Perspectives on Christian Initiation and the Catechumenate* (Notre Dame: University of Notre Dame, 1976), 1-6.

## Chapter 15. The Liminal Domain of War

1. Hedges, Chris, *War is a Force that Gives Us Meaning* (New York: Anchor, 2003).

2. Tick, Edward, *War and the Soul: Healing our Nation's Veterans from Post-Traumatic Stress Disorder* (Wheaton, Illinois: Quest Books, 2005), 45-62.

3. Brock, Rita Nakashima and Gabriella Lettini, *Soul Repair: Recovering from Moral Injury after War* (Boston: Beacon Press, 2013).

4. Owen, Wilfred, *The Collected Poems of Wilfred Owen*, ed. C. Day Lewis (New York: New Directions, 1963).

5. Mervyn Cooke, *Britten: War Requiem*, Cambridge Music Handbooks (Cambridge: Cambridge University Press, 1996).

6. Maria Mälksoo, "The challenge of liminality for International Relations theory," in *Review of International Studies* 38 (2012), 481-494, doi:10.1017/S0260210511000829, p. 492.

## Epilogue

1. Ronald E. Osborn, *Creative Disarray: Models of Ministry in a Changing America* (St. Louis: Chalice Press, 1991).

# Bibliography

American Psychiatric Association. 2013. *Diagnostic and Statistical Manual of Mental Disorders.* 5th Edition. *DSM-5*™ Washington, D.C.: American Psychiatric Association.

Ariete, Silvano. 1976. *The Intrapsychic Self.* New York: Basic Books.

Baird, William. 1980. *1 Corinthians and 2 Corinthians.* Atlanta: John Knox Press.

Bell, Catherine. 1992. *Ritual Theory, Ritual Practice.* New York: Oxford University Press.

Bellah, Robert N. 1995. "Religious Pluralism and Religious Truth," in *Reflections.* New Haven: Yale Divinity School.

Berman, Morris. 1981. *The Reenchantment of the World.* Ithaca: Cornell University Press.

Billig, Otto, B.G. Burton-Bradley, and Ellen Doermann. 1976. "Schizophrenic Graphic Expression and Tribal Art in New Guinea," in Joseph Westermeyer, ed., *Anthropology and Mental Health.* The Hague: Mouton Publishers.

Bollas, Christopher. 1987. *The Shadow of the Object.* New York: Columbia University Press.

Brock, Rita Nakashima and Gabriella Lettini. 2013. *Soul Repair: Recovering from Moral Injury after War.* Boston: Beacon Press.

Browning, Don. 1987. *Religious Thought and the Modern Psychologies.* Philadelphia: Fortress Press.

Carter, Warren. 1994. "Households and Discipleship: A Study of Matthew 19-20," in *Journal for the Study of the New Testament,* Supplement Series 103. Sheffield: Sheffield Academic Press.

Chaucer, Geoffrey. 1969. *The Canterbury Tales.* New York: Mentor and Plume Books.

Christiansen, Drew. 1995. "And Your Elders Will Dream Dreams: Aging, Liminality and the Church's Ministry," in Sanks and Coleman, ed., *Reading the Signs of the Times.* New York: Paulist Press.

Cohen, Erik. 1985. "Tourism as Play," in *Religion,* 15:305-314.

Cooke, Mervyn. *Britten: 1996. War Requiem* (Cambridge Music Handbooks). Cambridge: Cambridge University Press.

Crossan, John Dominic. 1991. *The Historical Jesus: The Life of a Mediterranean Peasant.* San Francisco: Harper Collins.

d'Aquili, Eugene, and Andrew Newberg. 1993. "Liminality, Trance, and Unitary States in Ritual and Meditation," in *Studia Liturgica,* 23, No. 1:2-34.

d'Aquili, Eugene, Charles Laughlin, Jr., and John McManus. 1979. *The Spectrum of Ritual: A Biogenetic Structural Analysis.* New York: Columbia University Press.

Douglas, Mary. 1966. *Purity and Danger.* New York: Frederick A. Praeger.

Douglas, Rees Conrad. 1988. "Liminality and Conversion in Joseph and Aseneth," in *Journal for the Study of the Pseudepigrapha,* No. 3:31-42.

Driver, Tom. 1991. *The Magic of Ritual.* San Francisco: HarperCollins.

Durkheim, Emile. 1915. *The Elementary Forms of the Religious Life.* New York: The Free Press.

Durrant, Michael. 1993. *Residential Treatment.* New York: W.W. Norton & Company.

Edgerton, Don. 1985. "Worship and Transformation," in *The Chicago Theological Seminary Register.* Chicago: Chicago Theological Seminary.

Eliade, Mircea. 1958. *Rites and Symbols of Initiation.* New York: Harper & Row.

——. 1959. *The Sacred and the Profane.* New York: Harcourt Brace Jovanovich.

——. 1960. *Myths, Dreams and Mysteries.* New York: Harper & Row.

——. 1963. *Myth and Reality.* New York: Harper & Row.

——. 1964. *Shamanism: Archaic Techniques of Ecstasy.* New York: Pantheon Books.

Epston, David, and Michael White. 1990. *Narrative Means to Therapeutic Ends.* New York: W.W. Norton & Company.

——. 1991. "Consulting Your Consultants: The Documentation of Alternative Knowledges," in *Experience, Contradiction, Narrative and Imagination: Selected Papers of David Epston and Michael White, 1989-1991.* South Australia: Dulwich Centre Publications.

Fishman, Robert. 1980. "Transmigration, Liminality, and Spiritualist Healing," in *Journal of Religion and Health,* Vol. 19, No. 3.

Foucault, Michel. 1988. *Madness and Civilization.* New York: Vintage Books.

Garcia, Luis F. 1994. Dissertation. *The Portrait of a Man: A Case Study of Lance Corporal Tirade's Liminal Transition and the Pastoral Counselor as a Guide Through Liminality.* Claremont: School of Theology at Claremont.

Gay, Volney. 1983. "Ritual and Self-Esteem in Victor Turner and Heinz Kohut," in *Zygon,* 18:271-282.

Hedges, Chris. 2003. *War is a Force that Gives Us Meaning.* New York: Anchor.

Horvath, Agnes, Bjorn Thomassen, and Harald Wydra. 2015. *Breaking Boundaries: Varieties of Liminality.* New York & Oxford: Berghahn Books.

Gerhart, Mary, and Allan Russell. 1994. *Metaphoric Process.* Fort Worth: TCU Press.

Gerkin, Charles. 1984. *The Living Human Document.* Nashville: Abingdon Press.

——. 1986. *Widening the Horizons.* Philadelphia: The Westminster Press.

Gilhus, Ingvild. 1984. "Gnosticism: A Study in Liminal Symbolism," in *Numen,* 31:106-128, July.

Giller, Pinchas. 1993. *The Enlightened Will Shine: Symbolization and Theurgy in the Later Strata of the Zohar.* Albany: State University of New York Press.

Goodwin, Lawrence. 1979. "Eucharist and Liminality," in *AFER,* Vol. 21. Eldoret, Kenya: AMECEA Pastoral Institute.

Green, Arthur. 1979. *Tormented Master: A Life of Rabbi Nahman of Bratzlar.* Tuscaloosa: University of Alabama Press.

Hall, James A. 1991. "The Watcher at the Gates of Dawn: The Transformation of the Self in Liminality and by the Transcendent Function," in Nathan Schwartz-Salant and Murray Stein, eds., *Liminality and Transitional Phenomena.* Wilmette, Illinois: Chiron Publications.

Hallstein, Ann. 1992. "Spiritual Opportunities in the Liminal Rites of Hospitalization," in *Journal of Religion and Health,* 31:247-254.

Inge, William Ralph. 1899. *Christian Mysticism.* New York: Scribner's.

James, William. 1958. *The Varieties of Religious Experience.* New York: The New American Library.

Jonas, Hans. 1958. *The Gnostic Religion.* Boston: Beacon Press.

Jonassen, Frederick B. 1991. "The Inn, the Cathedral, and the Pilgrimage of the Canterbury Tales," in *Rebels and Rivals.* Kalamazoo: Medieval Institute Publications.

Jung, Carl. 1938. *Psychology and Religion.* New York: Vail-Ballou Press.

Katz, Elihu and Daniel Dayan. 1985. "Media Events: On the Experience of Not Being There," in *Religion,* 15:305-314.

Kavanagh, Aidan. 1976. "Christian Initiation," in *Made, Not Born: New Perspectives on Christian Initiation and the Catechumenate.* Notre Dame: University of Notre Dame.

Kavanaugh, Kieran and Otilio Rodriguez, ed. 1964. *The Collected Works of St. John of the Cross.* Washington D.C.: Institute of Carmelite Studies.

———. 1976. *The Collected Works of St. Teresa of Avila.* Washington D.C.: Institute of Carmelite Studies.

Kobak, R. Rogers and David B. Waters. 1984. "Family Therapy as a Rite of Passage: Play's the Thing," in *Family Process.* Walwick, New Jersey: Family Process.

Kuhn, Thomas S. 1970. *The Structure of Scientific Revolutions.* Chicago: University of Chicago Press.

Lane, Beldon. 1988. *Landscapes of the Sacred.* New York: Paulist Press.

Levi-Strauss, Claude. 1966. *The Savage Mind.* Chicago: University of Chicago Press.

———. 1967. *Structural Anthropology.* New York: Anchor Books.

Lewis, Ioan M. 1971. *Ecstatic Religion.* Baltimore: Penguin Books.

Maack, Phillas. 1986. "Feminine Behavior, Radical Action," in *Signs: Journal of Women in Culture and Society,* No. 3:457-477.

Macnab, Francis. 1965. *Estrangement and Relationship.* Bloomington, Indiana: Indiana University Press.

Mälksoo, Maria. 2012. "The challenge of liminality for International Relations theory," in *Review of International Studies,* 38:481-494, doi:10.1017/S0260210511000829.

Mauck, Marchita B. 1979. "The Liminal Space of Ritual and Art," in John R. May, ed., *The Bent World: Essays on Religion and Culture.* Atlanta: Scholars Press.

McVann, Mark. 1988. "The Passion in Mark: Transformation Ritual," in *Biblical Theology Bulletin,* 18:96-101.

Moody, Christopher. 1986. "Students, Chaplaincy and Pilgrimage," in *Theology,* 89:440-447.

Moore, Robert. 1983. "Contemporary Psychotherapy as Ritual Process: An Initial Reconnaissance," in *Zygon,* 18:283-294.

——. 1991. "Ritual, Sacred Space, and Healing: The Psychoanalyst as Ritual Elder," in Nathan Schwartz-Salant and Murray Stein, eds., *Liminality and Transitional Phenomena.* Wilmette, Illinois: Chiron Publications.

Naisbitt, John. 1994. *Global Paradox.* New York: William Morrow and Company.

Nichols, J. Randall. 1985. "Worship as Anti-Structure: The Contribution of Victor Turner," in *Theology Today,* Vol. XLI, No. 4.

Odajnyk, Walter V. 1987. "The Meaning of Depression at Significant Stages of Life," in Louise Carus Madhi, ed., *Betwixt and Between.* La Salle, Illinois: Open Court Pub. Co.

Osborn, Ronald E. 1991. *Creative Disarray: Models of Ministry in a Changing America.* St. Louis: Chalice Press.

Owen, Wilfred. 1963. *The Collected Poems of Wilfred Owen,* ed. C. Day Lewis. New York: New Directions.

Patterson, Stephen J. 1993. *The Gospel of Thomas and Jesus.* Sonoma: Polebridge.

Pentikainen, Juha. 1979. "The Symbolism of Liminality," in *Religious Symbols and Their Functions.* Uppsala: Almqvist & Wiksell International.

Perdue, Leo. 1981. "Liminality as a Social Setting for Wisdom Instructions," in *Zeitschrift fur die Alttestamentliche Wissenschaft,* 93, No. 1:114-126.

Perry, John W. 1976. *Roots of Renewal in Myth and Madness: The Meaning of Psychotic Episodes.* San Francisco: Jossey-Bass Publishers.

Pruyser, Paul. 1976. *The Minister as Diagnostician.* Philadelphia: The Westminster Press.

Roberts, William, Jr. 1982. *Initiation To Adulthood.* New York: Pilgrim Press.

Ruiz, Jean-Pierre. 1992. "Betwixt and Between on the Lord's Day: Liturgy and the Apocalypse," in E. Lovering, ed., *The Society of Biblical Literature 1992 Seminar Papers.* Atlanta: Scholars Press.

Sered, Susan. 1989. "Rachel's Tomb: Societal Liminality and the Revitalization of a Shrine," in *Religion,* 19.

Shean, Glenn. 1979. *Schizophrenia: An Introduction to Research and Theory.* New York: University Press of America.

Silvermann, Julian. 1967. "Shamans and Acute Schizophrenia," in *American Anthropologist,* Vol. 69, No. 1.

Stein, Jan and Murray. 1987. "Psychotherapy, Initiation and the Midlife Transition," in Louise Cams Mahdi, ed., *Betwixt and Between.* La Salle, Illinois: Open Court Pub. Co.

Stifler, Kenneth, Joanne Greer, William Sneck and Robert Dovenmuehle. 1993. "An Empirical Investigation of the Discriminability of Reported Mystical Experiences Among Religious Contemplatives, Psychotic Inpatients, and Normal Adults," in *Journal for the Scientific Study of Religion,* Vol. 32, No. 4.

Stirrat, R.L. 1984. "Sacred Models," in *Man.* London: Royal Anthropological Institute of Great Britain and Ireland.

Stone, Howard. 1993. *Crisis Counseling.* Minneapolis: Fortress Press.

Taylor, Mark. 1986. "In Praise of Shaky Ground: The Liminal Christ and Cultural Pluralism," in *Theology Today* 43, No. 1:36-51.

Theissen, Gerd. 1978. *Sociology of Early Palestinian Christianity.* Philadelphia: Fortress Press.

Tick, Edward. 2005. *War and the Soul: Healing our Nation's Veterans from Post-Traumatic Stress Disorder.* Wheaton, Illinois: Quest Books.

Turner, Victor. 1967. "Betwixt and Between: The Liminal Period in Rites of Passage," in *The Forest of Symbols* . Ithaca: Cornell University Press.

———. 1969. *The Ritual Process: Structure and Anti-Structure.* New York: Aldine Publishing Company.

———. 1977. "Death and the Dead in the Pilgrimage Process," in *Religious Encounters With Death.* University Park: Pennsylvania State University Press.

———. 1983. "Body, Brain and Culture," in *Zygon,* Vol. 18, No. 3.

———. 1985. "Liminality, Kabbalah, and the Media," in *Religion,* 15:205-217.

Underhill, Evelyn. 1961. *Mysticism.* New York: Dutton.

Valantasis, Richard and Vincent L. Wimbush, ed. 1995. *Asceticism.* New York: Oxford University Press.

van Gennep, Arnold. 1960. *The Rites of Passage.* London: Routledge and Kegan Paul.

Welch, Claude. 1972. *Protestant Thought in the Nineteenth Century, Vol. I.* New Haven: Yale University Press.

Westermeyer, Joseph. 1976. *Anthropology and Mental Health.* The Hague: Mouton Publishers.

Zadra, Dario. 1984. "Victor Turner's Theory of Religion: Toward an Analysis of Symbolic Time," in *Anthropology and the Study of Religion.* Chicago: Center for the Scientific Study of Religion.

# Index

*Coming soon...*

# Crossing Thresholds

## *A Practical Theology of Liminality in Christian Discipleship, Worship and Mission*

### Rosemary Fairhurst and Nigel Rooms

Print ISBN: 978 0 7188 9346 0
PDF ISBN: 978 0 7188 4237 6
ePub ISBN: 978 0 7188 4239 0
Kindle ISBN: 978 0 7188 4238 3

A theological guide to the concept of liminality through multi-disciplinary lenses, demonstrating its value in theological reflection and formation and some of the key issues it raises for the mission of the contemporary church.

*Find more excellent titles in Paperback, Hardback, PDF and ePub formats on The Lutterworth Press website*

www.lutterworth.com